THE PEASANT COOKBOOK

BY MARIAN TRACY

Casserole Cookery *with Nino Tracy*
Care and Feeding of Friends
Cooking Under Pressure
More Casserole Cookery
Editor of Coast to Coast Cookery
East-West Book of Rice Cookery
Marian Tracy's Complete Chicken Cookery

MARIAN TRACY

THE PEASANT COOKBOOK

With illustrations by
MARGUERITE BURGESS

HANOVER HOUSE, GARDEN CITY, NEW YORK

Library of Congress Catalog Card Number 55–7026

Copyright ©, 1955, by Marian Tracy
All Rights Reserved
Printed in the United States
At the Country Life Press, Garden City, N.Y.
First Edition

INTRODUCTION

As living, and even existence, gets more and more complex in what may or may not be the best of all worlds, there is an increasing and pleasing tendency toward the simple and vivid things of life. There are bright peasant designs in clothes, dishes, furniture, fabrics, and foods. They fit into an informal way of living and entertaining and have the merit of having been tested by many centuries in many places.

These recipes are much-beloved ones from many countries and have been especially selected to fit our ways of cooking and eating, of entertaining without fuss or ceremony. None of those chosen requires ingredients not available in most large cities or that would startle or shock our simple and often prejudiced tastes. Basically many dishes are much the same, though each may be different in texture, cooking procedure, seasoning, and sometimes pleasantly unexpected in presentation. Chopped meat, for instance, is much the same everywhere, but Italian meat balls are robustly flavored, long-cooked, Danish are light, fluffy, and delicately seasoned. Both are delicious, as are the Swedish, Persian, and Roumanian, to name a few you can find here.

It is fascinating to attempt to puzzle out the way in which a dish crosses geographical and gastronomic borders, and wanders around the globe. It seems reasonable that there should be similar combinations of foods with slightly different emphases in the seasoning in places like the south of France, Spain, Portugal, and Italy, which all have ample supplies of olive oil, garlic, sweet peppers, anchovies, and sea food. But why should the tempura of Japan, which is properly not just shrimp but bits of meat and vegetables dipped in a batter and deep-fried, be, except for the accompanying sauce, so like the *fritto misto* of Italy halfway around the world? It is the

7

custom in Roumania as well as in Russia to sweeten tea with a spoonful of raspberry jam or lemon marmalade. I am told by a friend who was born long ago in Russia and also by a Norwegian friend that there is a special low-class delight, frowned upon by both their families, that they find almost irresistible, even now. It is to hold a lump of sugar in the mouth and drink coffee, blissfully letting it trickle through the sugar. Sugar in the cup never tastes quite as good, they tell me, still feeling a little guilty about it.

Cooks everywhere stir bits of this and that into eggs to give them more substance. What they add and the way they season it make the dish different, and the result is a Danish *aeggekage,* an Italian *frittata,* a Basque *piperade,* or the fiery Mexican *hueves rancheros.*

While the sturdy, nourishing, and varied dried legumes, which are plentiful and easily kept, are cooked in almost every country, each one cooks them its own way, and they are all good whether it is the vinegar-flavored but delicate Swedish beans, the buttery and garlicky Persian ones, the Roumanian ones beaten with lard until light, the large meaty Italian *fave* cooked with spinach, or the grand production that is the French *cassoulet.* Still, a good lusty split-pea soup is not so different whether it is eaten in Sweden, Holland, Denmark, or the province of Quebec.

Foods and seasonings vary, but food habits are much the same. Bits of meat or cheese are baked in large or small pieces of dough almost everywhere. The miners' lunch of a large meat turnover, called Cornish pasties, is not unlike the South American *empanadas* filled with meat and seasoned somewhat like mincemeat and served with coffee. The Swiss cheese pie, the Italian *pizza,* and the Provence *pissaladiera* are alike in principle. Although the dough and the fillings are different, the intent is the same.

Each country cooks lovingly and well the filling and fattening food that is its favorite starch. In Sweden the potatoes, which keep well in its cold climate, taste good in a pudding that is cooked with anchovies, herring, or smoked salmon. In Germany the potatoes are mashed or grated into dumplings and pancakes, or new potatoes are served swimming in bacon fat and with a pitcher of sour cream. Roumanians and Northern Italians cook and eat corn meal as enthusiastically and as often as our Southerners, and the Italians embellish it with as many sauces as they put on pasta. All

8

around the Mediterranean rice is cooked and served day in and day out for all parts of the meal in its many and delectable guises.

In most countries the food in the markets is seasonal, unlike our year-round plenty. Because this is so, they have their own ways of achieving a fresh or acid contrast to their daily foods. One touch, surprising to many Americans but somehow very good, is to serve large dill-flavored pickles as we would serve a salad. They are especially good with beans or any starchy dish. In many countries large handfuls of parsley are served in or with various dishes. It has good flavor and good nutrition, and can be encouraged to grow the year round almost everywhere.

While patterns of eating are conditioned by habit and what is available, the emotions are almost as important in determining what is eaten daily. Everyone knows that certain foods are pleasing or displeasing because of our associations with them and some foods are eaten because they mean security, some because they were once given as rewards for good behavior, some, like coffee, tea, or whiskey, mostly because they make one feel mature. Some foods are fetish foods that will cure all ailments and, therefore, presumably all problems and many eat yoghurt and wheat germ for just such reasons. There are foods that give one a feeling of prestige or elegance, such as caviar and champagne. All these foods are good in themselves—it is just that some of the reasons for eating or not eating them are restricting and sometimes even silly.

A book such as this could not have been done without the help of my friends of foreign background and the help of their friends who gave me much information and many recipes. Some of these were Nina Ayala, Madeline Timourian, Mrs. Stefan Irimescu, Elisabeth Fairer, Karin Fennow and her mother; Irma Rombauer, Marion Becker, Davoud Yonan, Julio de Diego, Lucy Glarner, Estanislao Fabres, Gertrude Li, Margaret Gerber, Mardi Ruvolo, Eleanor Felder, Norma Zamboni, and Rosemary Scheffreen; Jean Evans, Susan Esberg, Jean Lapolla and Marcel Perret.

MARIAN TRACY
Santa Fe, 1954

9

THE PEASANT COOKBOOK

Ghivech (Roumanian)

TIME: 2½ HOURS, NOT COUNTING SHOPPING TIME

This is, perhaps, the most spectacular and beautiful of all the ways of cooking vegetables and tastes as good and as different as it looks. The number of vegetables you use varies with availability. A lavish Roumanian hostess prides herself on the number of different vegetables she has used and, furthermore, will tell you so that you will know just how special an occasion this is. A really impressive ghivech may have from 12 to 18 different vegetables. There are some vegetables that are in all ghivech, one of the cabbages (cauliflower, broccoli, Brussels sprouts, or red or green cabbage) tomatoes, potatoes, carrots, onions, or two or three green vegetables such as peas, green beans, and then whatever other vegetables you can lay your hands on. The only ones never used are spinach, other cooked greens, and beets. This is not as extravagant a dish as it sounds, because just a handful of some of the vegetables is used. In some versions meat, preferably lamb or pork chops, is added at the last, but I like the vegetables alone. In order to cook and serve this it is necessary to have a large, shallow casserole, either earthenware or one of the enameled ironware that is so colorful and practical.

12

Menu: ROAST LAMB, BASTED WITH TARRAGON VINEGAR
GHIVECH
CHEESE AND FRESH PEARS
COFFEE

GHIVECH:

1 head cauliflower or a bunch broccoli, surplus leaves trimmed and stalks cut off
3 large potatoes, peeled and diced
4 carrots, scraped, sliced thin
1 eggplant, cut into large cubes with the peel left on
4 large tomatoes, quartered and seeds removed OR *1 large can Italian plum tomatoes, drained*
1 yellow squash, sliced thin but not peeled
4 or 5 medium-sized onions
1 cup fresh green peas
1 cup green beans, slivered or cut in pieces
1 green or red pepper, seeds removed, sliced thin
4 stalks celery, cut fine
2 cups soup stock
⅔ cup olive oil
4 or 5 cloves garlic, peeled (Roumanian version has much more)
1 tablespoon freshly chopped dill or mixed herbs
Lots of salt, little pepper

Parboil the cauliflower, potatoes, carrots about 15 minutes. Drain. Mix all the vegetables together, raw and cooked, in the casserole, pour in the soup stock, which should be heated with the olive oil and the garlic cloves. Sprinkle the top with the herbs. In a few parts of the country a bunch of white seedless grapes, pulled from the stem, are strewn around the top. This gives a delicate, acid touch that is very pleasing. Bake in a medium oven for 1½ hours or until all vegetables are fork-tender. Because this was usually baked in the village oven and then brought home, it is customary to serve this lukewarm. The flavors are better when it is not served hot from the oven. It is a good idea to finish it about ½ to 1 hour before dinner and let it cool slightly on top of the stove. Serves 6 to 8 generously.

New potatoes with bacon (kartoffel mit speck— German)

TIME: 45 MINUTES

When Irma Rombauer was a young art student in Germany, she wandered around attempting (as she puts it) to paint the dikes, windmills, and thatched houses of the northern region. Lunch was usually ordered in advance at some convenient farmhouse. With her companions she would enter the *Bauerstube,* or peasant general room, to find awaiting them great bowls of freshly boiled potatoes in their jackets, and diced bacon that had been cooked slowly so that it was swimming in fat. They peeled the potatoes, spooned the bacon over them, and topped the mound with some sour cream sprinkled with chopped chives. For dessert there was a Stollen, dark with raisins, currants, and citron, and coffee. We who always like a color and flavor contrast might accompany this simple yet savory meal with chilled cherry tomatoes or a crisp green salad.

Menu: KARTOFFEL MIT SPECK, SOUR CREAM, CHIVES, SALT AND
PEPPER
CHILLED CHERRY TOMATOES
STOLLEN (A RICH COFFEECAKE)
COFFEE

KARTOFFEL MIT SPECK:
2 *pounds new potatoes*
½ *pound bacon, cut in pieces*
½ *pint or more sour cream*
3 *tablespoons chopped chives*
Salt and pepper

Boil the potatoes in their jackets, drain, and keep warm. Cook the bacon slowly until pink and cooked but not crisp. Pour off some of the drippings, keeping just enough to flavor. Peel the potatoes and proceed as described above. Serves 4.

French Omelet

TIME: 30 MINUTES

No matter where you eat in France, what part of the country, or how fancy or how simple the restaurant, it is difficult to find a bad omelet. Perhaps this is because the French have so much respect for, and experience in, cooking eggs. If the eggs are fresh, and the heat is low and basic instructions followed, it is difficult to go wrong. There is much abracadabra about flipping and rolling omelets, but don't let it worry you. The French are apt, often as not, to serve them flat rather than rolled. They are just as tender that way and simpler to make. One important piece of every Frenchwoman's basic equipment is an omelet pan used for omelets alone. It is never washed out, just wiped out with a cloth and coarse salt, and their omelets never stick.

Menu: OMELET
ARTICHOKES WITH ONION AND DILL (see page 49)
FRENCH BREAD
STRAWBERRIES AND CREAM
COFFEE

OMELET:

4 eggs, slightly beaten
Salt
1 tablespoon butter

Melt the butter in the pan, add the eggs and salt, stir slightly, cook over a very low flame, tilting the pan from time to time so that the uncooked liquid runs under the cooked part. When one side is done, turn it over and cook the other side. When browned serve immediately. Some add to the omelet a little milk or cream for a rich version; others water for a more delicate one. Serves 2.

Cocido (Spanish)

TIME: ALL DAY COOKING; OVERNIGHT SOAKING

In Spain, as elsewhere, the ingredients of a cocido, or stew, vary from family to family and depend much upon the tastes, finances, and even the whim of the individual cook. Julio de Diego, who likes to cook as much as he likes to paint, says that this is a good, everyday version. For occasions when one wishes to be more lavish add uncooked ham in one piece, a blood sausage (available in groceries selling foreign foods and not half so revolting as it sounds to the squeamish), and half a chicken. The proper service of this dish is very impressive. First the broth, strained from the stew and flavored with saffron, is served with a spoonful of cooked rice in each bowl and garnished with croutons fried in olive oil. The second course consists of the garbanzos drained from the stew, accompanied by a vegetable (cooked separately) such as string beans, cabbage, or spinach dressed with hot olive oil flavored with garlic. (The garlic clove is heated in the oil and discarded before pouring on the vegetable.) As the last and most important course, all the meats are arranged decoratively on a platter, the chicken in the center surrounded by the cut-up pieces of meat. A bowl or small, fat pitcher of tomato sauce is passed around so that each may add it to whatever meat is desired. In this servantless country and period the stew may be served all at once from a tureen or great casserole into large, deep bowls. If served this way the meats should be cut up in the kitchen before transferring to the serving dish or pot.

Menu: COCIDO
FRENCH BREAD (FOR MOPPING UP JUICES)
FRUIT
COFFEE

COCIDO:

> 1 pound good stew meat, in one piece
> ¼ pound bacon in one piece
> 1 chorizo (*highly seasoned Spanish sausage available in Spanish or Mexican groceries*)
> 1 soupbone with marrow
> 1 pound chick-peas, or garbanzos, ceci (*all the same thing*) soaked overnight
> 4 or 5 large potatoes, peeled
> Saffron
> Salt and pepper

For the lavish version:

> ½ pound uncooked ham, in one piece
> 1 blood sausage, in one piece
> ½ chicken, in one piece

Sauce:

> 5 medium-sized tomatoes, cut in quarters
> 2 fat cloves garlic
> 2 tablespoons olive oil
> ½ teaspoon cumin, or comino, seed or 1 teaspoon orégano
> Cooked rice for the broth
> Cooked green vegetables (*string beans, cabbage, spinach*)

Wash all the meats and soupbone with hot water. Put all the meats in a pot of boiling water and let come back to a hard boil. Skim off the unsavory foam. Turn the heat down so the pot just simmers. Continue to skim off the foam until there is none. After ¾ hour add the soaked chick-peas, which have been just rinsed with hot water. Simmer for about 3 hours or until the garbanzos are tender. This will vary according to the age of the garbanzos and it is impossible to tell that until they are cooked. About 1 hour before the end add the potatoes. Remove the soupbone, leaving the marrow in the stew. Add the salt.

To make the sauce, simmer together all the ingredients until thickened and saucelike, at least ¾ to 1 hour. Strain and serve separately. Serves 6 to 8—this is the time you invite friends in.

17

Steak and kidney pie (English)

TIME: 1¾ HOURS

This is one of the best-beloved of all English dishes, even by those not usually enthusiastic about British gastronomy. Traditionally this is served with boiled potatoes. To Americans there might be more appeal, besides more nutrition, if the potatoes are boiled and served in their jackets.

Menu: STEAK AND KIDNEY PIE
BOILED POTATOES IN THEIR JACKETS
SALADE NIÇOISE (see page 70)
HOT BISCUITS
RED PUDDING (see menu, page 144)
COFFEE

STEAK AND KIDNEY PIE:

1 pound lean steak, either round or chuck, cubed
1 beef kidney, cut into pieces and the white removed
Flour
Salt and lots of black pepper
3 tablespoons oil
10 small white onions, peeled
Recipe for one pie crust
1 egg yolk

Dust the pieces of steak and the kidney lavishly with the flour. Season with the salt and pepper. On the next step the instructions vary a bit: some sauté the beef and kidney in the olive oil until browned on all sides; others put them into the casserole uncooked. Either way the meat and the onions are covered with water and simmered in a medium oven for about 1 hour or until the onions and steak are tender. By this time the flour on the meat should have cooked with the water until reduced somewhat miraculously to a smooth, thick, and lumpless gravy. Remove from the oven, put the pie crust on, pinching at the edges, and brush the top with egg yolk beaten with a little water and put back into a 400° oven for about 15 minutes or until the top is shiny and light brown. Serves 4 amply.

Italian fish stew (buridda)

TIME: 40 MINUTES

This mélange of sea food is simpler to prepare but also more lusty in flavor than the French bourride.

Menu: BURIDDA

FRENCH OR ITALIAN BREAD FOR MOPPING UP THE JUICES

RISOTTO MILANESE (see page 138) FOR THOSE WITH LIMIT-LESS APPETITES; NORMAL ONES WILL FIND THE STEW SUFFICIENT

TOSSED GREEN SALAD WITH FRENCH DRESSING (2 PARTS OLIVE OIL, 1 PART GARLIC VINEGAR, SALT AND PEPPER)

ZABAGLIONE OR COFFEE CUSTARD

COFFEE

BURIDDA:

⅓ cup olive oil

2 medium-sized onions, peeled and sliced

2 or 3 cloves garlic, peeled and minced

1½ pounds solid fish, cut in thick slices or chunks; bass or mackerel are good in this

1 dozen clams or mussels, in their well-scrubbed shells

½ cup dry white wine

Salt, if necessary, and pepper

Heat the olive oil in a large skillet. Add the onions and garlic and cook until pale yellow but not brown. Sprinkle with the parsley and lay the pieces of the fish on this. Cover and cook for about 10 minutes. Remove the cover, add the clams and/or the mussels in their shells, the white wine, salt, and pepper. Cover and cook for 5 minutes more. Serve immediately in large, hot soup bowls, shells and all. Serves 4.

Spiedini alla Romana (skewered bread and cheese, broiled or cooked over an open fire—Italian)

TIME: 30 MINUTES

This is a simple, frugal, and yet filling dish easily concocted, not only for a light, satisfactory meal, but for those sudden and unscheduled hungers. Start with an icy-cold gazpacho for an outdoor meal, then serve the spiedini hot from the grill. (Naturally it may be made inside, too.) For dessert have an important "made" dessert from a good bakery or one of the specialties of your own house.

Menu: GAZPACHO (see page 30)
SPIEDINI ALLA ROMANA
COLD WHITE WINE
IMPORTANT DESSERT
COFFEE

SPIEDINI ALLA ROMANA:

1 long loaf Italian or French bread, split in half and cut in chunks
2 large lumps of Mozzarella, cut in smaller chunks
Olive oil
Anchovy paste

Take long metal skewers and thread one chunk of bread, then a lump of cheese, then another chunk of bread, and so on, dividing the ingredients among the four skewers. Mix the olive oil with a little anchovy paste and brush over the loaded skewers. Place under a broiler, turning frequently until the bread is slightly toasted and the cheese soft and melting. Slide from the skewer onto individual plates. Serves 4.

Green pepper salad (Roumanian)

TIME: 1 HOUR

This makes a simple yet spectacular salad course. Unlike most salads, it may be and should be prepared ahead. It is easy to serve. All of which makes it just about perfect for buffet and outdoor entertaining.

Menu: CLAM CHOWDER IN SUFFICIENT QUANTITY FOR A MAIN
      COURSE
      HOT CORN-MEAL MUFFINS (INSTEAD OF THE TRADITIONAL
      CRACKERS)
      GREEN PEPPER SALAD
      KEY WEST LIME PIE
      COFFEE

GREEN PEPPER SALAD:
    8 medium-sized unblemished sweet green peppers
    1 cup olive oil or salad oil
    ⅓ cup red wine vinegar
    Salt and pepper

Bake or broil the peppers whole, turning from time to time until all sides are blistered so that you can peel off the skin. This will be only a few minutes. Skin the peppers carefully, leaving them whole. Blend the oil, vinegar, salt, and pepper, pour over the whole peeled peppers, and chill in the refrigerator. Serve ice-cold and drained. Save the dressing for another time. Serves 4.

21

Tío Pepe (black beans with garlic sauce—Spanish)

TIME: 24 HOURS WITH OVERNIGHT SOAKING, 10 HOURS IF SOAKED DURING DAY

Each country cooks its beans or dried legumes the very best way of all, I think as I try them, but then I really like all the good dried vegetables cooked so many, many ways. Julio de Diego, who told me how to make them this way, said, in answer to my astonishment, that a whole head of garlic is really mild when the head is cooked as a whole with just the outer wrappings removed. It is true, the garlic flavor and aroma are gentle as they permeate the beans. Both the black and white navy beans are traditional in this dish, but the color and meatiness of the black beans are more pleasing.

Menu: GAZPACHO (see page 30)
(see page 30)
TÍO PEPE
FRESH PEARS WITH CAMEMBERT CHEESE
COFFEE

TÍO PEPE:
> 1 pound dried black or white beans, soaked overnight
> 1 whole head garlic, the outside covering removed but still left in a cluster
> 4 strips bacon, cut in pieces
> 1 clove garlic, minced
> ½ cup olive oil
> 1 teaspoon cumin, or comino
> 1 tablespoon salt

Cook the beans, which have already been soaked in water overnight, in fresh water enough to cover, with the whole head of garlic, until tender. When the beans are done, the skin curls back when a few on a spoon are blown upon gently. Drain the beans, remove the head of garlic and discard, put into a bean pot or other deep earthenware casserole. Sauté the bacon briefly, and add to the pot. Sauté the minced clove of garlic in the olive oil until pale yellow but not brown. Strain from the oil, pour the oil, cumin, and salt onto the beans. Heat together long enough for the flavors to get acquainted, say about 20 to 30 minutes. Serves 4.

Bouillabaisse (French)

TIME: 45 MINUTES, NOT INCLUDING SHOPPING

The best-publicized and perhaps the best-loved of all fish mélanges, and one that causes most controversies among the purists. While the combination of fishes used in the true Marseilles version is not available here, this combination is very good, though the nostalgic ones will not be appeased.

Menu: BOUILLABAISSE
        LOTS OF FRENCH BREAD
        APPLES AND CAMEMBERT CHEESE
        COFFEE

BOUILLABAISSE:

There should be about four kinds of sea food of various types.

1 large onion, chopped
2 cloves garlic, chopped fine
½ cup olive oil
3 tomatoes, peeled, seeded, and quartered
1 tablespoon chopped fresh fennel, if available
1 bay leaf
¼ teaspoon thyme
*1 teaspoon saffron, soaked in ⅓ cup hot water, then
   strained*
Salt and 10 peppercorns
2 pounds firm fish, well cleaned, bass, smelt, and so on
*2 pounds soft fish such as salt-water perch, whiting, and
   so on*

Sauté the onion and garlic in the oil until pale yellow, adding the tomatoes, fennel, bay leaf, thyme, saffron water, salt, and peppercorns. Simmer 5 to 10 minutes. Add the fish, the firm ones first, and almost cover with water. Bring to a boil, turn heat down, and let simmer 12 to 15 minutes. After about 6 or 7 minutes add the more delicate fish. When the fish is tender and opaque, transfer it to a warm platter and serve as a separate and second course. Drain the broth, pour over slices of toasted bread in soup bowls. Serve immediately as the first course. Serves 4 to 6 lavishly.

Danish open-faced Sandwiches

TIME: DEPENDS

Many, pretty, and varied are the Danish open-faced sandwiches or
Smørrebrød. These sandwiches, each with its own garnish, a thin
slice of lemon or cucumber, decorative overlapping slices of
hard-cooked eggs, a sliced radish, a dollop of dark, quivering
meat jelly, or thin onion rings arranged chain fashion, and so on,
are served for dinners, late evening snacks, for workmen's lunches,
to the school children, or as party refreshments. The traditional
accompanying liquid, except for children, is a strong jolt of ice-
cold *akavit* with a beer chaser. The varieties of the sandwiches are
only limited by your ingredients and imagination, though they do
follow traditional patterns. The bread should be good dark rye or
pumpernickel. The Danish sour rye is as dark, but not as sweet, as
pumpernickel. It is sliced thin, the butter cold and barely spread-
able. The beef, roast pork, ham, or caraway-seed cheese, in slices
slightly larger than the bread, droops lavishly over it.

Some combinations are, more specifically: generous slices of
roast beef with a spot of freshly grated horse-radish and finely
chopped, cooked beets; herring, arranged side by side, with a
slanting line of finely chopped pickle; a large, thin slice of smoked
salmon, its beautiful color complemented by a middle frill of crisp
green lettuce; a fried fish fillet bedded on a piece of lettuce with
a spoonful of tartar sauce on top and, possibly, a thin slice of
lemon. Raw beef, with no fat at all, is scraped with the blunt side
of a knife and spread on the bread with a raw egg yolk nestled
cozily in an onion ring in the center.

Liver paste is spread on the rye and decorated sometimes with
a slanting line of radish slices, other times with crumbled crisp
bacon and sautéed mushrooms. Roquefort cheese is spread on the
bread and that, too, is decorated with a raw egg yolk, which
tastes much better than it sounds to the uninitiated. To eat, break
the yolk and spread it over all the cheese. Hot scrambled eggs,
sprinkled with tiny shrimps and chopped truffles on toast, are
another favorite. With our larger shrimp it would be best to chop
a few shrimp coarsely before sprinkling on the hot eggs and,
with the price of truffles here, sautéed mushrooms might add a

pleasant touch. Calf's liver is used with either sautéed onions, fried egg, or what we call sautéed mushroom and they call stewed. Thin, crisp bacon is sprinkled with the sautéed, or stewed, mushrooms on toast. Other times the bacon is arranged on a sandwich spread with cream cheese and topped with a fried egg. Freshly boiled tongue is embellished variously with asparagus dipped in mayonnaise, a fried egg, or just a dollop of good, clear meat jelly. Lobster is dressed with mayonnaise well seasoned with curry. Four boned anchovies are arranged on a slice of bread and topped with scrambled eggs sprinkled with finely cut chives.

These sandwiches are often followed by thin, delicate pancakes topped with vanilla ice cream and sometimes a spoonful of strawberry jam.

Red beans with butter sauce (Persian)

TIME: 12 TO 24 HOURS SOAKING THE BEANS; WITH CANNED BEANS
30 MINUTES WILL DO

Here one usually thinks of beans as baked in the New England
fashion, the red beans and rice of the South and Caribbean, or the
highly seasoned chile of the Southwest. In Iran, one of the oldest
civilizations, red beans are cooked and served this delicate and
savory way, according to Davoud Yonan, an artist who was born
there when it was still called Persia. He says that this is better
made with buffalo butter because it is more delicate than that made
from cow's milk. Also, to be authentic, the yoghurt should be dried
in balls in the sun, then pounded in a mortar with water added a
little at a time until a smooth paste is made. However, to me plain
cow's butter and yoghurt tastes very good. This menu uses the
traditional water cress for a spicy accent, but adds a baked slice
of ham and an open fruit pie to suit American ideas of what a meal
should be.

Menu: THICK SLICE OF HAM, BAKED
RED BEANS WITH BUTTER SAUCE
YOGHURT
WATER CRESS (NO DRESSING)
CORN-MEAL MUFFINS
OPEN-FACED BLUEBERRY TARTS
COFFEE

RED BEANS WITH BUTTER SAUCE:

*1 pound dried red kidney beans (or 2 cans without
sauce, well drained)*
2 medium-sized onions, chopped
2 plump cloves garlic, chopped
1 stick (¼ pound) butter, preferably unsalted
Salt and pepper
Paprika

Soak the beans overnight or for an equivalent time. Simmer until tender. Drain. The Persians mash the beans slightly but I rather like the plump, individual look of the beans. Sauté the onions and garlic in the butter until pale yellow and cooked, but do not brown. Add the well-drained beans, salt, pepper, and paprika and heat together briefly. This may be done in a casserole and kept in the oven until wanted. Serve with a crisp bowl of water cress and a fat pitcher or bowl of yoghurt. If this is used for a buffet supper, serve with a whole or half ham. Serves 4.

Eggplant Parmesan (Italian)

TIME: 4 HOURS

Sometimes Italians make this dish with the two cheeses and a plain marinara or plain tomato sauce. Other times they use with the cheeses the regular or usual Italian meat sauce cooked so long that you are not quite sure that there is meat in the sauce, except that it tastes very rich and good. This is made with the meat sauce. Some nights several cans of Italian tomato sauce may be used frugally and quickly instead of the meat sauce.

Menu: EGGPLANT PARMESAN

TOSSED GREEN SALAD WITH FRENCH DRESSING (2 PARTS OLIVE OIL, 1 PART GARLIC VINEGAR, SALT AND PEPPER)

FRENCH OR ITALIAN BREAD, CUT IN THICK SLICES

LEMON SOUFFLÉ OR PUDDING

COFFEE

EGGPLANT PARMESAN:

2 cloves garlic, chopped fine
1 onion, chopped fine
3 tablespoons olive oil
½ pound Italian sausage, either the sweet or the hot, removed from the skin, or 1 pork chop
1 pound chopped beef
1 teaspoon basil
1 teaspoon orégano
1 can Italian tomato paste
1 large can tomatoes, preferably the Italian plum
2 medium-sized eggplants
Flour
2 tablespoons olive oil
½ cup freshly grated Parmesan cheese
1 lump Mozzarella, cut in thin slices

The meat sauce, like most good Italian sauces, should cook for 3 or 4 hours. Sauté the garlic and onion in the olive oil. Add the sausage, or pork chop, and the chopped meat. Sauté until well browned. Add the basil, the orégano, the Italian tomato paste, the plum tomatoes, and about 1 cup water. Stir well and cook over a very low flame. Stir frequently with a wooden spoon. Add a little water from time to time if it starts to get too thick too soon. After 3 hours it should be fairly smooth and thick. If a pork chop was used, remove it from the sauce—this was just used for flavoring; if sausage was used, leave it in. Peel the eggplants, cut into thick slices, and put into a bowl of cold, salted water for about 1 hour until needed. Remove from the water, pat dry, flour, and sauté in the olive oil until brown on both sides. Drain on paper towels. Arrange one layer of sautéed eggplant in a casserole then a layer of the sliced Mozzarella, some of the Italian meat sauce, the plain tomato sauce, and a heavy sprinkling of the grated Parmesan cheese. Repeat until all the ingredients are used, ending up with the two cheeses on top. Bake in a 350° oven for about 20 minutes or until the cheeses have melted. Serves 4 to 6.

Filet Falso.

Deep Fry cubed Eggplant in fat mixed with the oil from canned Sardines.

Z. S.

Gazpacho (Spanish)

TIME: 1 HOUR FOR CHILLING

In Spain the farm workers are pampered by having this pungent soup brought to them in the field in cold earthenware jugs. Here it is good as a first course on a hot, hot day. It may be made ahead and is always chilled. Obviously with this there is no need for a salad.

Menu: GAZPACHO, WITH COLD WHITE WINE
    CHEESE AND MUSHROOM SOUFFLÉ
    FRENCH BREAD
    COFFEE CUSTARD AND THIN CHOCOLATE WAFERS
    COFFEE

GAZPACHO:

>2 *fat cloves garlic*
>1 *large onion*
>3 *tablespoons chopped parsley*
>1½ *teaspoons salt*
>3 *large tomatoes*
>1 *cucumber*
>1 *large green pepper*
>⅓ *cup olive oil*
>3 *tablespoons vinegar*
>1 *teaspoon orégano*
>½ *cup large dry bread crumbs*

Chop very fine or, even better, mash in a mortar the garlic, onion, and parsley with the salt. Chop the tomato, cucumber, and green pepper, of course removing the seeds and white membrane from the pepper first. Add the garlic and onion mixture and mash all together. Add the olive oil little by little, the vinegar, and the orégano and mix well. Divide into 4 soup bowls and chill thoroughly. Some recipes dilute this slightly with ice water, and you may do so, though this version doesn't. Just before serving, sprinkle each bowl with some of the breadcrumbs. Serves 4.

Fondue (Swiss)

TIME: 1 HOUR

This dish is for happy, blissful, and communal dunking. It is a production, pleasing and not really fussy. Each one spears a piece of bread with his fork. The first one dips it into the fondue, being careful not to lose the bread, and stirs leisurely until it is well coated. As the first takes his cheese-coated piece of bread from the pan and eats it from the fork, the next takes his turn stirring with his bread and so on. The fondue should be kept gently bubbling. This, of course, is for a light meal, lunch, say, or Sunday-night supper. A chafing dish or earthenware casserole is needed with an alcohol burner or an electric plate with an asbestos pad. Cold kirsch is the only liquor traditionally drunk with this meal.

Menu: SWISS FONDUE, WITH KIRSCH
FRENCH BREAD
SALAD: RAW VEGETABLES—CAULIFLOWERLETS, SLICED CARROTS, SLICED ONION, TOMATO, ALL MARINATED IN FRENCH DRESSING (2 PARTS OLIVE OIL, 1 PART VINEGAR, 1 TEASPOON DRY ENGLISH MUSTARD, SALT AND PEPPER)
FRUIT TART
COFFEE

SWISS FONDUE:

½ pound Switzerland Swiss cheese, finely cut or shredded (the domestic is the wrong texture)

1½ tablespoons flour

1 clove garlic

1 cup Neufchâtel wine or any dry white wine such as Rhine, Riesling, or Chablis

Salt and pepper, pinch nutmeg

1 loaf French or Italian bread or 4 hard-crusted rolls, cut in bite-size pieces, each with a piece of crust for flavor and firmness

3 tablespoons kirsch or, less traditionally, any unsweetened brandy such as applejack, slivowitz, cognac, or even light rum.

Dust the cheese with the flour. Rub the casserole with the cut clove of garlic. Pour in the wine and heat over a low flame in the kitchen. When it begins to show small bubbles, but before it boils, add the cheese, handful by handful, stirring all the while. Let each melt completely before adding the next. When the mixture bubbles gently, add salt, pepper, and nutmeg. Last stir in the kirsch and put over the alcohol flame or the electric plate, being careful to remember the asbestos pad. Now go into your act. Serves 4.

Piperade (Basque)

TIME: 45 MINUTES

Basically this is a rich and savory sauce with eggs added at the last minute almost as an afterthought.

Menu: SLICED COOKED HAM, WITH COLD CHABLIS
PIPERADE
TOSSED GREEN SALAD WITH A BLAND FRENCH DRESSING
(3 PARTS OLIVE OIL, 1 PART VINEGAR, SALT AND
PEPPER)
FRENCH BREAD
CAMEMBERT CHEESE
COFFEE

PIPERADE:

2 tablespoons olive oil
2 sweet peppers, preferably one red and one green, seeds
removed and cut in thin rings
1 clove of garlic, chopped
1 small onion, chopped
2 tomatoes, chopped and seeds removed
4 eggs

Sauté the peppers in the olive oil with the garlic and the onion. Cook slowly until they are somewhat intermingled, tender and squashy, add the tomatoes, salt, and pepper, and cook very slowly, stirring the mixture occasionally until it is somewhat like a purée. Break into the sauce one by one the whole raw eggs and stir quickly over the fire. The heat of the sauce will cook the eggs almost immediately. The result should be a frothy sauce with the eggs practically indistinguishable. Serves 4.

Baked potatoes with toasted cheese (Swiss)

TIME: 1½ HOURS

The food that fascinated me first in a book was the meal of dark bread, toasted cheese, and goat's milk, described so lovingly in *Heidi*. At that time I had never tasted any of the good dark breads, the sour ryes, or the sweet, moist pumpernickels. But I had tasted and disdained the white grocery-store bread. I wondered at Heidi's stupidity in saving this in her closet during her homesick stay in the city. Possibly that white bread was a good, crusty French type. This Swiss dish has much of the savor and simplicity I had imagined in Heidi's meal. It is good food to eat on a picnic, an intimate one, with a fire to bake the potatoes and to lend its magic to good, leisurely conversation.

Bake large, mealy potatoes, the skins well scrubbed and buttered, in the hot coals of the fire. When done break open with fingers well protected with a towel. Let steam and cool a few minutes while toasting some good Cheddar cheese over the fire. As it melts, spoon it bit by bit onto the potatoes. Conventional palates, if found at such a meal, will feel uneasy without some such addition as thick slices of a fine Canadian-style bacon, perhaps the hickory-smoked from Stroudsburg, Pennsylvania, some small cherry tomatoes to pop in the mouth in one bite, and deep-fried pies to put a period to this bliss. To make these pies, cut 3-inch circles of pie dough, put a spoonful of a good apple butter or homemade raspberry jam on each circle. Fold over and pinch together carefully. Fry in deep fat until golden and crunchy. If I were young, and knew where to get it, I would like some home-churned buttermilk with this meal. Now I'd settle for some chilled Vouvray, one of my favorite of all white wines, with almost a sparkle. Naturally this meal may be cooked and eaten in greater comfort, and even more pleasurably, before one's own fireplace.

Turkish chicken pilaf

TIME: 1 HOUR

This is a little different from most pilafs in that the chicken is added raw and cooked along with the rice.

Menu: TURKISH CHICKEN PILAF
SWEET AND SOUR GREEN BEANS (see menu page 132)
HOT DROP BISCUITS (A GOOD READY-MIX WILL DO)
OPEN-FACED CHERRY TARTS
COFFEE

TURKISH CHICKEN PILAF:
½ cup (1 stick) butter
1 large onion, chopped
1½ cups raw chicken, cut from the bones in strips, or diced in large pieces
Cooked chicken giblets, diced (boil everything except the liver, which should be sautéed)
Salt and pepper
½ teaspoon dried thyme
1½ cups uncooked rice
3 cups chicken broth
⅓ cup chopped walnuts

Melt the butter and sauté the onion and chicken strips in it. Add the cooked giblets and the liver cut in pieces, salt, pepper, thyme, and rice. Cook the rice in the fat until pale yellow but not browned. Add the chicken broth, cover, and cook for 20 to 30 minutes or until all the liquid is absorbed. With this amount of butter it will not dry out. Add the walnuts, stir in well, and serve. Serves 4.

Dutch red cabbage and apples

TIME: 2 HOURS

On the continent, where people take their vegetables seriously, even cabbage has prestige, especially when cooked this way.

Menu: COLD SLICED TONGUE
DUTCH RED CABBAGE AND APPLES
RYE BREAD WITH CARAWAY SEEDS
PUMPKIN PIE
COFFEE

DUTCH RED CABBAGE AND APPLES:
3 tablespoons butter
1 small red cabbage, shredded
2 tablespoons wine vinegar
3 cooking apples, cored and diced but not peeled
Salt and pepper
1 tablespoon sugar

Heat the butter in a heavy skillet, add the cabbage, vinegar, apples, salt and pepper, and sugar. Cover tightly and cook over low heat for about 1½ hours. Sometimes a few tablespoonfuls of a tart jelly, say currant, is added to the cabbage and allowed to melt. Serves 4.

37

Fresh tenderloin of pork (svinemørbrad med abrikoser—Swedish)

TIME: 1¾ HOURS

The Scandinavians treat the raw foods they have, which are good but not varied according to our ideas, with loving care. Surprisingly this dish is presented and served somewhat with the same accompaniments as a curry.

Menu: SVINEMØRBRAD MED ABRIKOSER
HOT, FLUFFY RICE
SHREDDED COCONUT, SLIVERED ALMONDS, CHUTNEY, SHARP PRESERVED GINGER, AND SO ON
FRESH PLUMS AND CRÈME CHANTILLY (THE DELICATELY TANGY SWEDISH CREAM CHEESE)
COFFEE

SVINEMØRBRAD MED ABRIKOSER:

2 onions, chopped fine
½ pound fresh mushrooms (less will do, if too costly)
2 fresh (definitely not smoked) tenderloins of pork, diced
3 tablespoons butter
1 can chicken soup
A few tomatoes
1 large jar or can apricots (should be firm-fleshed, small)
Heavy cream (about ½ to ⅔ cup)
Salt and pepper

Cook the onions in a little water until tender. Drain. Sauté with about ¾ of the mushrooms (chopped or sliced) in butter in a good pot, preferably iron. Add cleaned and diced meat and brown well. Pour in soup somewhat diluted by ⅓ can. Add skinned and seeded tomatoes. Simmer for about 1 hour with the seasonings added. Slice remaining mushrooms and add with apricots. Simmer about 15 minutes more. Stir in enough cream to thicken. Serve with rice and condiments suggested above. Meat in the pot, rice on the side, other things in small dishes. Serves 4 generously.

38

Lamb stew (shorbi—Persian)

TIME: 2 HOURS

Davoud Yonan, an artist (all artists are good cooks—it's another creative outlet for them and besides they have or will take the time), still cooks the same dish he ate in Persia years and years ago.

Menu: SHORBI, WITH PINOT NOIR OR OTHER DOMESTIC BURGUNDY
  SALAD: GARDEN LETTUCE WITH FRENCH DRESSING (2 PARTS OLIVE OIL, 1 PART VINEGAR, SALT AND PEPPER)
  APRICOT BETTY (MADE JUST LIKE BROWN BETTY BUT WITH STEWED DRIED APRICOTS)
  COFFEE

SHORBI:

  2 *pounds lamb shoulder, cut in stew-sized pieces*
  2 *medium-sized onions, chopped*
  Butter or lamb fat
  1 *pound potatoes, peeled and cut into odd shapes (red new potatoes are best)*
  6 *whole hot green peppers (if not available, either fresh or in cans, use the whole sweet peppers—the flavor will be good but not the same)*
  1 *pound green beans*
  3 *medium-sized tomatoes, cut in quarters*
  Salt, paprika, black pepper

Sauté the meat and onions in butter or fat from the lamb until the meat is browned and the onions pale yellow. Transfer to stew pan, Dutch oven, or deep casserole. Barely cover the meat with boiling water. Simmer over low heat or in slow oven for 1 hour. When the meat is tender, add the potatoes, green peppers, green beans, and tomatoes. Cook until the vegetables are tender, about ½ hour or more. Serves 4.

Mamaliga with cheese (Roumanian)

TIME: 1¼ HOURS

Mamaliga, the staple food of Roumania, is corn meal mush or polenta in other languages and other countries. It is served in many simple and flavorful ways, all good. Layered with butter and grated cheese and baked until rich, golden, and gooey, and then topped with poached eggs, this perfect food is fit for the gods or, somewhat immodestly, me.

Menu: CANADIAN BACON, BAKED IN A WHOLE PIECE
MAMALIGA WITH CHEESE AND POACHED EGGS
COLD MARINATED STRING BEANS WITH SHARP FRENCH DRESSING (HALF OLIVE OIL AND HALF VINEGAR, SALT AND PEPPER)
RED RASPBERRIES WITH CREAM AND THE THIN, THIN GINGERSNAPS THAT COME IN LONG TINS

MAMALIGA:
1 cup yellow corn meal
1 tablespoon salt
1 stick (¼ pound) butter, preferably unsalted
1 cup freshly grated Kascaval, Parmesan, or Switzerland Swiss cheese
4 freshly poached eggs

Heat 4 cups water (1 quart) until boiling. Sprinkle a handful of corn meal into the water, stirring constantly, adding a small amount of corn meal from time to time. Turn the flame down very low each time before adding the corn meal or it will go plop over everything. When as thick as you like, say about the consistency of mashed potatoes, turn out the flame and keep stirring until very smooth. The Roumanians use a special wooden stick, carved in individual designs, somewhat like a broomstick or French rolling pin, but a sturdy wooden spoon will do. With a spoon spread a layer of mamaliga on the bottom of a greased casserole. Dot with pieces of butter and sprinkle generously with the grated cheese. Repeat such layers until the ingredients are used, ending up with cheese and butter on top. Bake briefly in the oven until the cheese is melted and bubbling. Just before serving, slide the poached eggs on top in a pleasing arrangement. Each person is served a portion of the mamaliga with an egg. Serves 4.

Baked codfish (bacalhao fresco à Portuguesa)

TIME: 1 HOUR

After you cross the border from Spain into Portugal the food looks much the same, but the seasoning is as mild as the climate. Butter is used more often than oil and somehow the food seems richer.

Menu: BACALHAO FRESCO À PORTUGUESA
       THIN, BITTER STALKS BELGIAN ENDIVE, NO DRESSING
       FRENCH BREAD
       MACAROONS
       COFFEE

BACALHAO FRESCO À PORTUGUESA:

1 medium-sized eggplant, cut in slices
¼ cup olive oil
3 large onions, sliced
3 tablespoons capers (rinse the salted ones), chopped
1 cup cooked rice
½ teaspoon cumin seed, mashed in a mortar or with some blunt instrument
2½ to 3 pounds fresh codfish steaks
4 tomatoes, peeled and chopped or 1 (No. 1) can tomatoes
3 tablespoons butter
3 tablespoons lemon juice
Salt and pepper, paprika

Sauté the eggplant in the olive oil, drain on paper towels, and transfer to a long baking dish. Sauté the onion rings until pale yellow, strew over the eggplant. Mix capers and rice with the cumin seed. Spread the seasoned rice over the onion and eggplant and arrange the pieces of codfish on top. Add the tomatoes and 1 cup water. Dot with pieces of butter and sprinkle with lemon juice, salt and pepper, and paprika. Cover and bake in a 325° oven for ½ hour. Remove the cover and bake 10 to 15 minutes more or until the codfish is an opaque white and flaky. Serves 6.

Ratatouille (French Provençal)

TIME: 50 MINUTES

A sautéed and less pretentious variant of a vegetable stew than the baked Roumanian *ghivech*, lustier too. In a ghivech the many vegetables tend to gentle the ones inclined to predominate. In this all have a forceful appeal.

Menu: SPIEDINI ALLA ROMANA (see page 20)
        RATATOUILLE
        FRESH PEARS
        COFFEE

RATATOUILLE:
    ½ cup olive oil
    2 onions, peeled and chopped
    2 fat cloves garlic, minced
    2 or 3 tomatoes, cut in pieces
    2 green peppers, cut in thin pieces and tops and seeds removed
    1 large eggplant, cut in cubes but not peeled
    1 zucchini or yellow squash, sliced thin
    Bay leaf
    3 slices bacon, diced and cooked
    Salt and pepper
    Diced, cooked lamb if desired

Sauté the onion and garlic in the olive oil, add the tomatoes, green pepper, eggplant, zucchini, and bay leaf. Cook over a low flame, stirring around until all the vegetables are sautéed. Add the bacon, salt and pepper, cover, and simmer over a low flame 15 or 20 minutes. Remove the bay leaf and serve immediately. Serves 4 to 6.

Swiss cheese tart

TIME: 1½ HOURS

Day after day the Swiss make a meal, and a good one, they think, on pie and coffee for lunch and sometimes other meals. A fruit pie as the main part of a meal, no matter how decoratively the fruits—apple, plum, or peach—are arranged in slanting rows on the flat circles of dough, seems like a dessert to us. We feel guilty in the face of constant barrages of nutritional admonitions. They have other pies that do seem more reasonable to us—this Swiss cheese one and a strange but good one made with chopped spinach and bacon.

Menu: COLD BORSCHT (see page 146)
SWISS CHEESE TART
COLD COOKED GREEN BEANS, MARINATED IN FRENCH DRESS-
ING WITH CHOPPED BLACK WALNUTS
HOT BROILED PEACH HALVES FILLED WITH COLD ALMOND-
FLAVORED WHIPPED CREAM
COFFEE

SWISS CHEESE TART:

   piecrust for 9-inch pie
   ½ pound Switzerland Swiss cheese, grated
   1 tablespoon flour
   1 cup milk or light cream
   3 eggs, well beaten
   Salt and pepper

Line pie dish with pastry. Dust the cheese with flour. Sprinkle cheese in pie dish. Mix beaten eggs with milk and seasoning. Pour over the cheese. Bake 15 minutes in hot oven (400°), reduce heat to slow oven (300°), and bake 30 minutes more, or until knife inserted comes out clean. Serve hot. May be made ahead and warmed. Serves 4.

Sauerbraten (German)

TIME: 4 DAYS

To those who like their beef rare most pot roasts seem rather tired and nondescript-tasting affairs. There is, however, something about sauerbraten with its sweet and sour sauce, long marinating, and potato dumplings that seems like a good and entirely different dish. Somehow, somewhere, someone started adding a few gingersnaps to the sauce, which taste very good, but cause the purists such acute pain that they have been left out of this version.

Menu: SAUERBRATEN
KARTOFFEL KLOESSE (see page 48)
COLESLAW
GERMAN APPLE CAKE
COFFEE

SAUERBRATEN:

2 cups beef bouillon
1 cup tarragon vinegar
2 tablespoons chopped parsley
2 teaspoons salt
½ teaspoon peppercorns
2 tablespoons dry English mustard
3 pounds beef, bottom round or eye roast, larded if the butcher will do it
Garlic
3 tablespoons butter or other fat
6 tablespoons flour
1 cup sour cream

Heat but do not boil the bouillon, vinegar, and seasonings. Put the meat in an earthenware crock or bowl and add this mixture. It should come to about half the height of the meat. Turn the meat once a day. Let it stand at least 3 days. Some like it to stand 8 to 10. Remove the meat from the marinade, rub the meat with garlic, and dredge with flour. Heat the butter in a Dutch oven or heavy pot and brown the meat on all sides. Add the marinade, which has been reheated, cover tightly, and cook over low heat. Simmer slowly for 2 or 3 hours. When tender, remove from the pot and thicken the juices with the flour mixed with enough water to make a thin paste. Cook until smooth, add the sour cream, heat until warm but do not let boil. Serve with the roast and kartoffel kloesse. Serves 6 to 8 generously.

Potato dumplings (kartoffel kloesse—German)

TIME: 1½ HOURS

The kartoffel kloesse are the light tender potato dumplings served with roasts and gravy in Germany. One of the best versions has toasted bread cubes inside.

Menu: ROAST PORK AND GRAVY
KARTOFFEL KLOESSE
TANGERINE SLAW (SHREDDED CABBAGE, TANGERINE SEGMENTS WITH SOUR-CREAM DRESSING—1 CUP SOUR CREAM, 1 TABLESPOON LEMON JUICE, SALT AND PEPPER, AND ½ TEASPOON DRY MUSTARD; MIX TOGETHER AND CHILL WELL. NATURALLY THIS IS NOT A GERMAN SLAW, BUT GOOD WITH A HEAVY MEAL)
RED PUDDING (see menu, page 144)
COFFEE

KARTOFFEL KLOESSE:
6 or 8 medium-sized potatoes boiled in their jackets, peeled, and riced or grated
2 egg yolks
Salt
Nutmeg, freshly grated
⅔ cup flour, or more
Toasted white bread cubes

Mix the riced or grated potatoes with the egg yolks, salt, a sprinkling of nutmeg, and the flour until the mixture sticks together. Make into balls about the size of a tennis ball and poke 3 or 4 of the toasted cubes into the center of the potato ball. Drop into boiling salted water and cook about 10 minutes (about 3 minutes after they come to the top). Remove one from the liquid and cut open. If the center is dry, they are sufficiently cooked. If cooked too long, the balls will fall apart and become soggy. Serves 4.

Artichokes with onion and dill (Armenian)

TIME: 1½ HOURS

On the other side of the Atlantic artichokes are served more casually than we do and more often. They are cooked in many, many more ways. This is a flavorful variation on the salad course.

Menu: PAN-FRIED HAM
PAPANASI (see page 71)
ARTICHOKES WITH ONION AND DILL
RED PUDDING (see menu, page 144)
MACAROONS
COFFEE

ARTICHOKES WITH ONION AND DILL:
4 large artichokes
8 very small onions
½ cup olive oil
2 lemons
1 tablespoon sugar
Salt and white pepper
Chopped fresh dill

Prepare the artichokes by cutting off the sharp tips and removing the choke with a knife. Scrape out the fuzzy part, being careful not to touch the good meaty part. Rub all over with half a lemon and boil the artichokes and onions in a pint of water with a sliced lemon until the onions and artichokes are tender. Drain and arrange the artichokes and onions in a shallow casserole. Sprinkle with the dill, salt, pepper, and olive oil. Add about a half inch of water, cover, and cook over a low heat for about 1 hour. Drain, chill. Serve with strained cooking liquid. Serves 4.

Lucy Glarner's chestnut and cabbage dish (Northern European dish)

TIME: 2 HOURS

The inhabitants of Belgium, Holland, Germany, Denmark, and, possibly, Switzerland all cook variations of this dish.

Menu: KNACKWURST OR KALBASSA (THE POLISH SAUSAGE) COOKED
AND SERVED SEPARATELY
CHESTNUT AND CABBAGE DISH
RYE BREAD
CHERRY COBBLER
COFFEE

CHESTNUT AND CABBAGE DISH:
1 pound chestnuts
1 small red cabbage, cut in wedges
4 green apples, cored, peeled, and quartered
4 onions, sliced thin
2 tablespoons olive oil
Salt and pepper

Cut deep crosses on the chestnuts. Cook in boiling water 25 minutes, until tender. Drain, peel, and skin. Sauté the onions in the oil. Put the chestnuts, cabbage, apple, and onions in a Dutch oven or baking dish with about half a cup of water and the seasonings. Cover and cook for about 1½ hours. Serves 4 to 6 robustly.

French boiled-beef salad

TIME: 1 HOUR CHILLING TIME

This is a traditional French hot-weather salad, usually made from the beef in the pot-au-feu the second day and is almost a meal in itself. Some families serve it with lukewarm poached eggs on top, which taste very good no matter how odd it sounds to Americans.

Menu: HOT MUSHROOM BOUILLON
       FRENCH BOILED-BEEF SALAD
       RASPBERRY TART
       COFFEE

FRENCH BOILED-BEEF SALAD:
   Lettuce leaves
   Sliced cold boiled beef (naturally roast beef can be used
      too, though not traditional)
   Diced cooked beets
   Diced cooked vegetables from the pot-au-feu
   French dressing (2 parts olive oil, 1 part vinegar, and the
      mashed yolks of 3 hard-cooked eggs)
   4 lukewarm poached eggs

Line the salad bowl with the crisp lettuce leaves, then with slices of the meat, the vegetables arranged decoratively inside that. Mix the dressing with the hard-cooked egg yolks, pour over, and chill. Just before serving arrange the poached eggs, which have been allowed to come to room temperature, on top. Serves 4.

Pot-au-feu (French)

TIME: ALL DAY

Theoretically and traditionally this is the pot that sits on the back of the fire, assuming that you have a coal fire. It is the French version of a pot roast, their way of cooking meat that needs long, moist simmering. In France, however, it is presented differently from the way it is here. The broth is served first with a piece of toast covered with grated Parmesan cheese in the bottom of the soup bowl, then the boiled beef is served as the main course, surrounded by the vegetables and accompanied by pickles and coarse salt. The next day the same meat and vegetables are either reheated or else made into a boiled-beef salad.

Menu: BEEF BROTH WITH TOAST AND PARMESAN CHEESE
BOILED BEEF
PICKLES AND COARSE SALT
TOSSED GREEN SALAD, WITH FRENCH DRESSING (2 PARTS
OLIVE OIL, 1 PART VINEGAR, SALT AND PEPPER)
FRENCH BREAD
CAMEMBERT CHEESE AND MORE BREAD
COFFEE

POT-AU-FEU:

3 pounds lean beef chuck or breast or round
1 marrowbone
Chicken necks, wings, and gizzards
1 bunch carrots, peeled and quartered lengthwise
1 pound turnips, peeled and quartered lengthwise
1 bunch leeks, white part only
1 stalk celery, cut in 1-inch pieces
12 peppercorns
2 cloves garlic
4 onions, chopped
Salt and pepper
Bay leaf
⅓ cup finely chopped parsley

Put the meat, marrowbone, and chicken parts in a deep, heavy pot, add seasonings and water to cover. Bring to a boil, skim foam off, bring to boil again, and skim until there isn't anything to skim. Simmer for about 4 hours or until the meat is almost tender, add the vegetables and cook 1 hour more. Remove the marrowbone, add the marrow to the pot. Discard the chicken parts—they are just for flavor. Either serve our usual way or the French way as described above. Many versions add potatoes and/or cabbage, cooked separately, but the cabbage conflicts with the delicate flavor. Serves 4 generously for 2 days.

Biftec a lo pobre (Chilean)

This was a workman's dish not very long ago in Chile, and is given more to shock you than for instruction. It reminds one of the story of the days in Maryland when terrapin was so plentiful that there were laws passed limiting the number of times a week slaves could be forced to eat it.

Menu: BIFTEC A LO POBRE WITH ONIONS
       FRENCH-FRIED POTATOES
       COFFEE

BIFTEC A LO POBRE:
>   2 large onions, shredded fine
>   ½ stick (⅛ pound) butter
>   Fillet of beefsteak or sirloin

Sauté the onions in the butter until they are soft, mushy, and almost indigestible. Transfer the onions to a dish and sauté the steak on both sides in the butter until the desired doneness. Spoon the onions generously over the sautéed steak, serve with French fries, and remember that this was recently a workman's lunch.

Kasha (Balkan)

TIME: 50 MINUTES

To my prejudiced mind kasha is the best of any of the daily starches, with more flavor, more nutrition, no tedious preparations. Cooked the usual way, it is a frugal, everyday dish. This is a much-embellished *kasha,* which is cracked buckwheat.

Menu: SAUTÉED CHICKEN LIVERS
      KASHA
      BROILED GREEN TOMATO SLICES
      SALT STICKS
      ORANGE SOUFFLÉ
      COFFEE

KASHA:

3 tablespoons butter or preferably chicken fat
1 medium-sized onion, chopped
1 cup kasha, medium ground
2½ cups chicken broth
2 tablespoons dried mushrooms, soaked in chicken broth
Salt and pepper

Sauté the onion in the fat. Add the kasha, stirring until well colored and almost parched. Put in a pot with the chicken broth, boiling hot, cover, and cook 20 to 25 minutes or until tender. Remove cover, add the mushrooms, which have been soaked in stock, drained, and cut in pieces. Stir and fluff with a fork. Top with sautéed chicken livers. Serves 4.

Poppy-seed noodles, Dutch style

TIME: 30 MINUTES

This is a pleasing addition to anyone's culinary repertoire.

Menu: SLICED TONGUE WITH CRANBERRY SAUCE (MELT ONE CAN
OF WHOLE CRANBERRY SAUCE WITH 1 TABLESPOON
GRATED LEMON PEEL AND ½ TEASPOON CINNAMON)
POPPY-SEED NOODLES
WATER-CRESS SALAD WITH FRENCH DRESSING (4 PARTS
OLIVE OIL, 1 PART GARLIC VINEGAR, SALT AND PEPPER)
MELBA TOAST
APPLE PIE WITH CHEDDAR CHEESE
COFFEE

POPPY-SEED NOODLES, DUTCH STYLE:
3 tablespoons butter
3 tablespoons poppy seeds
½ cup slivered almonds, blanched and roasted
1 tablespoon lemon juice
1 package (8 ounces) broad egg noodles, cooked in salted
  boiling water, then drained
Salt and cayenne pepper

Melt the butter and add the poppy seeds, slivered almonds, and lemon juice. Pour over the hot noodles and toss together. Serve very hot to 4.

Tamale pie (Mexican)

TIME: 2 HOURS

Tamales baked pie-fashion are definitely a lazy adaptation of the stuffed cornhusk, which is the authentic tamale. I don't know just where or when this inertia set in, but certainly it is better for city dwellers who may not always have access to good fresh cornhusks. However, the semi-purist (a real one would grind his own corn and prepare the chiles with his own hands, burning them with the fiery pods) may put a spoonful of this corn-meal mixture and a spoonful of this meat mixture on each corn husk, tie both ends, and steam them.

Menu: TAMALE PIE
SALAD WITH SLICED AVOCADO AND GRAPEFRUIT SEGMENTS
MELON BALLS CHILLED IN WHITE WINE
COFFEE

TAMALE PIE:
2 pounds pork or beef, cut in stew-sized pieces
3 cloves garlic
3 eight-ounce cans tomato sauce
1 eight-ounce bottle or can Mexican red chile sauce
Salt and pepper
1 small can ripe olives, chopped (nice but not obligatory)
½ box yellow corn meal

Simmer the pork or beef with the peeled cloves of garlic in a little water until tender, about 50 minutes to 1 hour. Remove garlic, add tomato sauce and red chile sauce. If the red chile sauce is not available in a Mexican food store near you, use another can of tomato sauce with a large amount of seasoning added, say 2 tablespoons chile powder, 1 teaspoon orégano. Dump in the chopped ripe olives. Again, the purist would make you bother with the olive pits. Meanwhile, while the meat is simmering in its sauce for about 20 minutes, cook the corn meal according to the directions on the box, stirring until smooth and stiff. Put half the corn-meal mixture in the bottom of an earthenware casserole, spread the meat and sauce mixture on top of the corn-meal layer, and top with the rest of the corn meal. If both mixtures are cooled slightly first, this procedure is simpler. Bake 1 hour in a 350° oven. Serves 4 to 6.

S'chee (Russian)

TIME: 4 HOURS

S'chee, or Russian cabbage soup, is similar to, and has about as many variations as, borscht. About the only difference is that in this soup cabbage instead of beets is the identifying ingredient. Almost any combination of vegetables is used, but there must be cabbage.

Menu: S'CHEE
> FRENCH BREAD
> LEMON MERINGUE TARTS
> COFFEE

S'CHEE:

> 1 head cabbage, cut in wedges and stalks removed
> 2 carrots, scraped and sliced
> 2 stalks celery, cut in pieces, leaves and all
> 1 turnip, peeled and quartered
> 6 cups beef bouillon
> 1 can Italian tomato paste
> Salt and pepper
> 2 onions, peeled and sliced
> 1 clove garlic
> 3 tablespoons bacon fat
> 3 medium-sized potatoes, peeled and quartered
> Sour cream
> Chopped fresh dill, if possible
> Chopped fresh parsley

Simmer the cabbage, carrots, celery, and turnips in the bouillon. Add the tomato paste, salt and pepper. Simmer for 2 or 3 hours. Sauté the onions and garlic in the bacon fat and add to the soup with the potatoes. Cook for about ½ hour longer. Serve in a large tureen with a bowl of sour cream on the side, with the dill and parsley to sprinkle on top. Serves 6 to 8.

Roumanian chopped meat (parjoale)

TIME: 40 MINUTES

The dill adds a delicate and different flavor to this Roumanian dish.

Menu: PARJOALE
     WHIPPED POTATOES WITH LOTS OF BUTTER AND CREAM
     DILL PICKLES (ROUMANIANS USE THESE OFTEN AS AN ACID
       TOUCH TO THE MEAL INSTEAD OF A SALAD)
     HOT POPPY-SEED ROLLS (BROWN-AND-SERVE KIND)
     APPLES WITH A GOOD SHARP CHEDDAR CHEESE
     COFFEE

PARJOALE:
> *1½ pounds chopped chuck*
> *2 eggs*
> *½ hard roll (or 2 slices stale bread) soaked in milk and squeezed out*
> *Salt and pepper*
> *1½ tablespoons finely chopped dill*
> *Bouillon*
> *Flour*
> *¼ cup butter or Crisco*

Mix the meat, eggs, moistened bread, salt and pepper, and dill together. Moisten with the bouillon until fluffy. Make into rolls 2 inches long and 1½ inches wide and 1½ inches thick. Dust lightly with flour and sauté in the hot oil. Serves 4.

Italian meat balls with tomato sauce

TIME: AT LEAST 4 HOURS

Now Italian meat balls are one of the most robustly seasoned of all chopped-meat concoctions, as anyone knows who has eaten even the cheap table d'hôte in a small Italian restaurant. This recipe, which is Jean Lapolla's version of her family's recipe, is particularly savory, both meat balls and sauce. She says that what gives the sauce its special flavor is the long cooking and the pork. When it is available, she adds a piece of Italian sweet sausage (removed from the skin) to the sauce during the long cooking. Other times she adds one lone pork chop, which is fished out before serving.

Menu: ITALIAN MEAT BALLS WITH TOMATO SAUCE AND PASTA
MIXED GREEN SALAD WITH FRENCH DRESSING (2 PARTS OLIVE OIL, 1 PART VINEGAR, SALT AND PEPPER)
ITALIAN OR FRENCH BREAD
RUM CAKE
COFFEE

MEAT BALLS:

1 pound chopped round or chuck beef
7 slices cubed bread, preferably stale, moistened with water
½ small onion, chopped fine
⅓ cup finely chopped parsley (about ½ bunch)
⅓ cup raisins
¼ cup freshly grated Parmesan or Romano cheese (the Romano is apt to be less salty these days)
1 or 2 whole eggs (2 make the meat balls more moist and tender)
Salt and pepper
Olive oil

Mix ingredients thoroughly and roll into balls about the size of a lemon. Poke the raisins in firmly—if any are on the outside they get hard. Brown on all sides in a skillet, the bottom barely covered with olive oil, but do not let them get a crust or they will be tough. Put into sauce which has been cooking for about ½ hour and continue cooking for about 3 hours more.

SAUCE:

> 1 small onion, chopped
> 1 clove garlic, chopped fine
> 3 tablespoons olive oil
> 1 large can tomatoes, preferably the Italian plum tomatoes, which are sweeter. Strain before adding to the pan.
> 1 can Italian tomato paste, 4 paste cans water
> ½ pound Italian sausage removed from the skin or 1 pork chop
> ⅓ cup finely chopped parsley
> 1 teaspoon orégano
> 1 teaspoon salt
> Pepper

Brown the onion and garlic in the oil, transfer to a large pot, and add the tomatoes, tomato paste, water, sausage or pork, parsley, and seasonings. Let cook over low heat about 3½ hours. Stir slowly from time to time with a wooden spoon, adding more water if needed. At the end of the time the sauce should be rich and thick, but not too thick to pour over the pasta. Have a large kettle of water boiling and just before serving dinner add the pasta. The various shapes take different times and somehow have different proportions to the sauce. The spiral pasta is one of the prettiest though the regular spaghetti is the most easily obtainable. Serves 6 generously.

Herring salad (German)

TIME: 1¼ HOURS, INCLUDING CHILLING TIME

Herring salad, a German dish, is almost a meal in itself for us if not for them. Traditionally the sauce is made with the milt from the fish. This version from a German-born woman uses a mayonnaise thinned with beet juice.

Menu: HERRING SALAD, BEER
       RYE BREAD WITH CARAWAY SEED
       CHEESECAKE
       COFFEE

HERRING SALAD:

- 4 *Iceland herring, soaked overnight*
- 1 *pound cooked veal, cut into pieces*
- 4 *medium-sized beets, cooked, peeled, diced, and the juice saved*
- 3 or 4 *apples, peeled, cored, and diced*
- 1 *stalk celery, chopped*
- 4 *hard-cooked eggs, yolk and white chopped separately*
- 4 *sweet pickles, chopped fine*
- 2 *tablespoons capers*
- 1 *cup mayonnaise*

Drain the herring, skin, bone, and cut into small pieces. Mix with all the ingredients except the capers, 1 egg, 1 beet, and 1 pickle. Thin the mayonnaise slightly with beet juice. Mix with the chopped ingredients and pat into a mound in a salad bowl. Chill. When ready to serve, divide the top into quarters with capers set in lines. Decorate one quarter of the salad with finely chopped beet, one quarter with finely chopped egg yolk, one quarter with finely chopped egg white, and the fourth quarter with the finely chopped pickles. Serves 4 to 6.

Green beans with potatoes, Swiss-fashion

TIME: 1½ HOURS

This is a day-in-and-day-out dish the Swiss eat happily.

Menu: GREEN BEANS AND POTATOES, SWISS-FASHION
      FRENCH BREAD
      RED PLUM TART
      COFFEE

GREEN BEANS WITH POTATOES, SWISS-FASHION:
    2 slices bacon, chopped
    1 medium-sized onion, chopped
    1 clove garlic, chopped
    1 pound green beans, slivered or broken in pieces
    ¼ pound salt pork, diced and scalded
    10 small new potatoes, scraped, or 5 medium-sized ones, peeled and quartered

Sauté the bacon and pour off most of the fat, leaving a thin film in the bottom of the skillet. Cook the onion and garlic in the fat, add the beans and 1 cup water or, less traditionally but flavorfully, 1 cup bouillon. Bury the pieces of salt pork in the beans, add the potatoes, cover, and cook together for about 1 hour. Frankfurters, the garlic kind, are often skinned and added to this dish. Allow 1 per person. Serves 4.

Italian lentil soup (zuppa di lenticchi)

TIME: 1½ HOURS

The Italians have a simple way of giving a meatless soup rich flavor as if from meat. The trick lies in cooking the vegetables in oil before adding to the lentil soup.

Menu: ZUPPA DI LENTICCHI
FRENCH OR ITALIAN BREAD
CUCUMBER AND ONION ASPIC WITH MAYONNAISE
APRICOT BAVARIAN CREAM
COFFEE

ZUPPA DI LENTICCHI:
1 cup lentils
¼ cup olive oil
1 medium-sized onion, chopped
1 clove garlic, minced fine
2 ribs celery, stalks and leaves chopped
⅓ cup finely chopped parsley
2 tablespoons tomato paste, diluted with ⅓ cup water
Salt and pepper
Grated Parmesan cheese

Cook the lentils in 6 cups of boiling salted water for about an hour. Heat the oil in a skillet and sauté the onion, garlic, celery, and parsley until deep brown. Add to the pan the lentils diluted with the tomato paste, salt and pepper. Simmer until the lentils are tender, adding more liquid if necessary for a sloshy consistency, perhaps 20 minutes or more. This is served in large, warmed soup bowls with the cheese sprinkled on top. It is a lusty meal in itself for 4 people.

Swedish omelet (flåskpannkaka)

TIME: 50 MINUTES

When the Swedish people make what they call an omelet, there is nothing temperamental about it, nor is it variable. According to a Swedish friend, this is the way it is always made and it is hard to make a mistake. Traditionally this is served with lingonberries, the Swedish cranberries, but our whole-cranberry sauce, or any tart jelly, jam, or marmalade will do. It is a good dish for a late and leisurely Sunday breakfast, lunch, or for a late, impromptu supper. This menu is planned for lunch.

Menu: GAZPACHO (see menu, page 30)
     FLÅSKPANNKAKA
     HOT BISCUITS (BUTTERMILK ONES THAT COME IN A TUBE)
     RICOTTA (THE ITALIAN COTTAGE CHEESE) SWEETENED,
         MIXED WITH HEAVY CREAM, CITRON, AND SHAVED BIT-
         TER CHOCOLATE
     COFFEE

FLÅSKPANNKAKA:
> 8 *slices bacon, cut in 1 inch pieces*
> 6 *eggs*
> 4 *tablespoons flour*
> 2 *cups milk*
> 1 *teaspoon salt*
> *Pinch white pepper*

Cook the bacon slowly until crisp, pour off most of the fat, leaving a thin film on the bottom of the skillet. Meanwhile beat the eggs with a rotary beater until light and fluffy, adding the flour a little at a time and beating until it is well blended. Add the milk and seasoning and beat some more. Pour over the hot fat and bacon and put into a medium oven, 375°, for about 35 minutes or until brown and puffy and slightly firm in the middle. Serve in the skillet at the table with lingonberries or other tart jam. If your skillet is copper or one of European enamel-covered ironware, it will look much better. Serves 4 generously.

Fish paprikash (Hungarian)

TIME: 1 HOUR

While it is not true that the Hungarians put paprika in everything, it does turn up in dishes delectably often. This dish, when made in Hungary, which has no seaport, is concocted with fresh-water fish. It tastes equally good made with a non-oily salt-water fish.

Menu: FISH PAPRIKASH
　　　BOILED POTATOES
　　　LEAF-LETTUCE SALAD WITH SLICED CUCUMBER, FRENCH
　　　　　DRESSING (3 PARTS OLIVE OIL, 1 PART VINEGAR, SALT
　　　　　AND PEPPER)
　　　STRAWBERRY FRITTERS (DIP FIRM WHOLE STRAWBERRIES
　　　　　IN FRITTER BATTER AND DEEP FRY)

FISH PAPRIKASH:
　　　2 tablespoons butter
　　　2 large onions, chopped fine
　　　1 teaspoon Hungarian paprika
　　　Salt
　　　½ cup white wine
　　　*1 pound fish fillets, cut in serving portions, authentically
　　　　such fresh-water fish as perch or carp*

Sauté the onions in the butter in a heavy saucepan until transparent. Add the paprika, salt, wine, and a half cup of water. Cover and simmer for about 30 minutes. Add the fish and simmer for 10 to 15 minutes more. When the fish is opaque, transfer to a serving platter and strain the sauce from the pan over the fish. Spoon the fish and sauce over the boiled potatoes.

Onion soup (soupe à l'oignon gratiné—French)

TIME: 40 MINUTES

This day-in-and-day-out soup that many Americans make is often their first approach to French cooking. Many of the French think it best to use water as the liquid, to get the full impact of the onion flavor. This somehow seems much too penurious to Americans who prefer to use beef bouillon or stock. Either way is good and either way is authentic. It is necessary that it be served in individual soup bowls with a thick slice of French bread on top, heavily loaded with grated Swiss or Parmesan cheese. This is put under the broiler or in the oven for 5 minutes or more until the cheese melts and spreads into a wonderfully golden crust that is hard to get your spoon through.

Menu: SOUPE A L'OIGNON GRATINÉ
AEGGEKAGE (see page 168)
SPICED CRAB APPLES WITH MACAROONS
COFFEE

SOUPE A L'OIGNON GRATINÉ:
3 tablespoons butter
2 large or 3 medium-sized onions, peeled and sliced thin
5 cups water or beef bouillon
Salt and pepper
6 thick slices French bread
⅓ cup grated Parmesan or Swiss cheese

Sauté the onions in the butter until tender and pale gold but not brown. Transfer to a soup pot with the water or the bouillon, salt and pepper. Bring to a boil and simmer 15 to 20 minutes. Pour into earthenware bowls that look somewhat like small bean pots and add a piece of bread heavily laden with grated cheese to each bowl. It will be simpler if all the bowls are put on a cooky sheet and put under the broiler or in the oven all at once rather than one by one. Brown in a hot oven for 5 minutes and serve immediately. Serves 4.

Cornish pasties (English)

TIME: 2 HOURS

This most portable of meat pies is a fine old English dish to make ahead, to take on a picnic, for a buffet dinner, or to put uncooked in the freezer to be freshly baked later on for just you and the family. It was originally, and still is, the regular lunch of the Cornish miners.

Menu: CORNISH PASTIES

　　　SALAD: CHICORY, DICED TOMATOES, AND ONIONS, FRENCH DRESSING (2 PARTS OLIVE OIL, 1 PART VINEGAR, SALT AND PEPPER)

　　　FRESH STRAWBERRIES AND FRESH OR FROZEN PINEAPPLE CHUNKS

　　　COFFEE

CORNISH PASTIES:

　Pastry:

　　　2 cups flour
　　　2 tablespoons lard
　　　1 teaspoon salt
　　　½ cup suet

68

Filling:
¾ pound beef, diced
3 potatoes, peeled and diced
1 turnip, peeled and diced
1 onion, peeled and chopped
Salt and pepper

Cut the lard into the flour sifted with salt. Mix with two knives or pastry blender. Grind the suet in a meat grinder and add to the mixture. Stir in a little ice water gently, mixing less than you think reasonable (it varies according to the moisture in the air and the flour). Roll out and cut into 4 large squares. Put a quarter of the meat and vegetable mixture on half of each square, filling a triangle. Fold the vacant triangle over the filled half and pinch together. Bake in a 325 degree oven for about 1 hour. Serve hot, lukewarm, or cold, but not chilled. Serves 4.

Salade niçoise (French)

TIME: 10 MINUTES, CHILL 30 MINUTES

While it is true the French make the most, and best, of all tossed green salads, there are other ones very good and yet not so well known—such as this. It uses robust ingredients that predominate in the South of France as well as Spain and Italy, though the French assemble them a little differently.

Menu: SWISS CHEESE TART (see page 44)
      SALADE NIÇOISE
      RED WINE
      FRENCH BREAD
      COFFEE

SALADE NIÇOISE:

    3 tomatoes, peeled and sliced
    2 boiled potatoes, peeled and diced
    ½ cup slivered, cooked string beans
    ½ cup black olives, preferably the salted kind that come in tubs
    1 tablespoon capers
    ⅓ tin fillet of anchovy, cut in pieces
    French dressing (4 parts olive oil, 1 part vinegar, salt and pepper)

This salad is at its decorative best when arranged to please the eye. There should be an outer circle of the sliced tomatoes with the diced potatoes heaped in the center, the string beans sprinkled over them and the black olives, anchovies, and capers sprinkled over all in such a way that the whole is a pleasant and colorful composition. Sprinkle the salad with the well-blended French dressing and chill until ready to serve, though this chilling business is probably American nonsense. Serves 4 to 6.

Pot cheese dumplings (papanasi—Roumanian)

TIME: 45 MINUTES

These dumplings, fragile in texture and delicate in flavor, are an important dish, an impressive contribution to a meal, not just something dropped into a stew almost as an afterthought.

Menu: PAN-FRIED HAM
       PAPANASI
       CUCUMBER SALAD (see page 159)
       STEWED PEARS WITH BITTER-CHOCOLATE SAUCE
       COFFEE

PAPANASI:

1 carton pot cheese (cottage cheese is too moist), pushed through strainer
4 eggs, separated
4 heaping tablespoons flour (most unscientific, but these are Roumanian directions that work)
Salt and pepper
3 tablespoons sweet butter
¼ cup bread crumbs
1 cup heavy cream (good but not essential)

Mix the pot cheese, egg yolks, flour, salt and pepper together. Whip the whites until stiff and fold gently into the cheese mixture. Drop by spoonfuls into rapidly boiling water. Cook about 5 minutes. Drain and put in a casserole with butter and bread crumbs. Add 1 cup heavy cream if desired, cover tightly, and put in a medium oven for 15 minutes and they will puff up prettily. They may also be fried and put in heavy cream. Serves 4.

Chicken stew (cazuela—Chilean)

TIME: 3 HOURS

This dish is half stew and half soup. In Chile it is served as a first course at midday on Sunday. We, being more delicate and more limited in our capacities, find this a meal in itself. The pumpkin and corn are the touches that indicate its Latin-American origin. South American pumpkin is much like ours in flavor, though not exactly the same. There is a special skill to eating the pieces of corn in a South American stew. Spear the small pieces of cob at the end with a fork, then bring the fork close to the mouth and eat the corn from the cob in the usual way. It is a trick that my Chilean friend's American wife hasn't mastered yet.

Menu: CAZUELA
BOWL OF CRISP WATER CRESS
FRENCH BREAD
CRÈME BRÛLÉE OR ANY OTHER CUSTARD
COFFEE

CAZUELA:

1 stewing fowl (5 to 6 pounds) cut up as for frying
Flour
Olive oil
Bouquet garni (bay leaf, orégano, parsley, thyme)
6 to 8 potatoes, peeled but left whole
½ pound string beans, broken into small pieces
½ pound fresh peas
1 small pumpkin, peeled, seeded, and cut into 3-inch squares
½ cup uncooked rice
2 ears corn, cut in 2-inch pieces
Salt and pepper
1 raw egg
¼ cup finely chopped parsley

72

Flour the pieces of fowl and sauté in the oil. Drain and put in a heavy pot with cold water to cover. Add the bouquet. Bring to a boil, turn down, and simmer, never letting it come to a boil again. From time to time skim off the fluff that comes to the top until there isn't any left to skim. After an hour add the potatoes and cook until tender, about 40 to 50 minutes. About 30 minutes after adding the potatoes add the string beans, fresh peas, and pumpkin. Cook 10 to 15 minutes more and add the rice. My Chilean friend removes all the vegetables and chicken at this time and cooks the rice in the broth, but it is not absolutely necessary. Cook the rice until tender, about 15 minutes. After about 10 minutes add the pieces of corn, salt and pepper, and the vegetables and meat if they were removed. Heat them together for a few minutes. Remove from the stove, let cool slightly. Break in the raw egg and stir very fast until smooth. The egg should thicken the gravy, done the right way. Serve some of each food with the thickened broth in warm soup bowls and sprinkle with parsley. Serves 6 to 8.

Grilled, skewered fish (baluck shish kebab—Armenian)

TIME: 10 MINUTES BROILING, 5 TO 6 HOURS STANDING, OR OVERNIGHT

Not so long ago nomad people around the Mediterranean skewered and cooked their food on their swords over an open fire because that was the way they lived. This was their usual way of cooking and eating rather than an act to put on outdoors, with the host wearing a chef's cap. They cooked not only meat but also fish in this fashion, preferably with fresh bay leaves between the chunks of fish. Fresh bay leaves being for the most part unavailable, such places as the Golden Horn in New York cook the fish deliciously with pieces of green pepper interspaced with the fish.

Menu: BALUCK SHISH KEBAB
BULGOUR WITH LEBAN (see page 212)
ROUMANIAN CUCUMBER SALAD (see page 159)
FRENCH BREAD
LEMON SHERBET
COFFEE

BALUCK SHISH KEBAB:
2 pounds codfish, halibut, swordfish, or any other firm fish
¼ cup lemon juice
1 bay leaf
3 green peppers, cut into 1½-inch squares
⅓ cup olive oil
Salt and pepper

Cut the fish into 1½-inch chunks. Sprinkle with the lemon juice and crumbled, dried bay leaf and let stand for 5 or 6 hours or overnight. Turn from time to time to make sure that every bit is covered with the lemon juice. When ready to cook, thread long skewers with a piece of the fish and the piece of green pepper, then a piece of fish and one of green pepper, and so on until the skewers are loaded. Brush with olive oil. Sprinkle with salt and pepper and put under a broiler. Broil about 10 minutes in all, turning the skewers over once or twice. The fish should be opaque and flaky by now and the pepper burned around the edges but still crisp. To serve, push the fish and green pepper off the skewer onto a deep, warm small platter. Serves 4 to 6.

Sukiyaki (Japanese)

TIME: 1 HOUR

Sukiyaki might be called a Japanese stew, being a concoction of meat and vegetables cooked together. There is, however, no lengthy cooking in which each food takes on the flavor of another. In this the cooking is so brief and the appearance of each food so decorative and distinct that each retains its own identity and crispness. It is a good show-off dish. All the preliminaries can be made way ahead and the brief cooking performed before an admiring audience. At the Miyako restaurant in New York the sukiyaki is cooked at each table. This particular combination of easily obtainable ingredients was given to me by a Japanese artist. At the Miyako bamboo shoots sliced the long way and tofu, the bean custard, cut in inch squares, are added to the dish for a pleasing and authentic touch. Japanese stores carry them.

Menu: SUKIYAKI
RICE WITH SHOYU (SOY) SAUCE
LEMON MERINGUE PIE
TEA

SUKIYAKI:

The amounts and proportions vary according to capacities.

2 tablespoons butter

2 onions, sliced thin

Boneless raw chicken, sliced, or uncooked rib roast, sliced paper-thin

Thin stalks asparagus, or thin strips zucchini, or green beans slivered

Celery, cut in thin strips

Green pepper, cut in rings and seeds removed

Green onions, cut diagonally

Bouillon

Soy sauce

Tomato, cubed

Mushrooms, sliced through the cap

1½ tablespoons flour or cornstarch, with enough water added to make a medium paste

Salt and pepper

Melt the butter in a large, heavy skillet over a hot fire. Put in the onion, meat (if chicken), celery, green pepper and cook until the meat is sautéed and the vegetables are half cooked. Add just enough bouillon to cover the bottom of the pan. Add the soy sauce, tomato, mushrooms and cook about 3 minutes. Thicken with the flour or cornstarch if desired. The artist thickens, Miyako doesn't. When beef is used, it is added at the last. The vegetables are pushed to one side of the pan and the beef is cooked slice by slice in that space, being turned over after ½ minute. Serve from the pan.

Baked omelet (frittata—Italian)

TIME: 50 MINUTES

This Italian version of a baked omelet may be concocted from almost any amiable combination of vegetables that are around.

Menu: FRITTATA

SLICED TOMATOES SPRINKLED WITH FINELY CHOPPED PARSLEY

FRUIT

COFFEE

FRITTATA:

⅓ cup olive oil

2 green peppers, cut in pieces, seeds and membranes discarded

⅓ cup sliced fresh mushrooms

5 eggs, beaten until fluffy

Salt and pepper

3 tablespoons grated Parmesan cheese

Heat about 2 tablespoons of the oil in a skillet and sauté the peppers until tender and slightly browned. Add the mushrooms and cook briefly. Let cool. Add to the fluffy beaten eggs with the salt and pepper and the cheese. Pour into another skillet that has been heated with the rest of the oil. Cook over a hot flame until cooked around the edges but still soft in the middle. Place under the broiler or in the oven until brown and firm. Serve cut in wedges. Serves 4.

Irish soda bread

TIME: 2 HOURS

The best of all Irish food, and I say this somewhat bitterly as a veteran or victim of many an Irish meal specially planned for the press, is Irish soda bread. Good, fresh, homemade bread is good in any land, but this is wonderfully good and wonderfully simple to make. There is the fun of kneading the bread, but none of the fuss of handling yeast, which frightens so many so unnecessarily.

SODA BREAD:

> *4 cups sifted flour*
> *1 teaspoon salt*
> *1 teaspoon sugar*
> *1 teaspoon baking soda*
> *Enough buttermilk to mix*

Put the sifted flour, salt, sugar, and baking soda into a bowl and make a dent in the middle. Pour in a little buttermilk, mix with the fingers and add enough more to make a fairly firm but not dry dough. The amount of buttermilk needed will vary according to the humidity. On damp days the flour absorbs moisture from the atmosphere and therefore less is needed in the dough. Turn out onto a floured board and knead lightly. To knead you pull the dough toward you and then push out with the bottom of your palm or the heel of your hand. Pull the dough toward you again and repeat this several times until it feels smooth and satiny. Pat into a round loaf and cut across on the top so that it will not crack in baking. Brush with milk and bake in a 450° oven 40 to 45 minutes. It is done when it sounds hollow when tapped. Sometimes about 1 tablespoon of caraway seeds is added to this. Other times ½ cup currants is mixed in the bread. Serve hot or cold with practically anything. Traditionally this is baked in a skillet but almost any round, darkened pan will do. With one too shiny it is not easy to get a good brown.

Broiled Roumanian meat balls (Mititei)

TIME: 2 HOURS

These sausagelike meat balls are best made ahead, chilled in the refrigerator long enough for the flavors to "set," then allowed to come back to room temperature before broiling. These are particularly good for outdoor broiling. With the *iahnie de fasole* and green pepper salad this typical Roumanian meal (typical, that is, except for the brownies) may be served for an outdoor or buffet meal both simply and well.

Menu: MITITEI

IAHNIE DE FASOLE (see page 136)

GREEN PEPPER SALAD (see page 21)

BROWNIES

COFFEE

MITITEI:

2 pounds chopped lean chuck
Bouillon
2 cloves garlic, chopped fine
Salt and pepper
Dried thyme

Marinate the meat in the bouillon and mix with the fingers until it is fluffy but not wet. Add the garlic, salt and pepper. Chill in refrigerator 1 hour. Let stand ½ hour at room temperature. Make into sausage or cigar-shaped rolls. Sprinkle with dried thyme and broil until the desired doneness. Serves 4.

Pan Bagna (French Provençal)

TIME: NO TIME AT ALL

This is a wondrously savory workman's lunch much like our Italian Hero sandwiches or the Poor Boy sandwiches in New Orleans without the meat and cheese.

Menu: PAN BAGNA
      TINY CHERRY TOMATOES
      CHEESE
      COFFEE

PAN BAGNA:

French bread, about a foot for each person, or one of the Pepperidge Farm French loaves freshly baked
3 tablespoons olive oil, if onions and pepper are sautéed
2 large onions, peeled and sliced
2 green peppers, cut into strips and seeds removed
Black olives (Italians leave the seeds in their flavorful wrinkled black olives)
Anchovies
More olive oil

The bread is split and filled lavishly with the onions and peppers, either sautéed in olive oil or raw, and the black olives and anchovies. Sprinkle with more olive oil. It is eaten blissfully and messily in your hands with some good red wine. Naturally this would be *vin ordinaire.*

Noodles Alfredo (Italian)

TIME: 30 MINUTES

Often bored by one-dish cookers who went on and on, pretentiously and tediously, about how they made their spaghetti sauce, I listened with delight the first time, rather long ago, I heard about these noodles. I think that the excellence of this dish is in its simplicity and in the quality of the ingredients. For this use the very best noodles, hand-made from good durum wheat, and sometimes even make them yourself. Search out in your city or town the very best unsalted butter, and a good piece of Parmesan cheese to be grated just before preparing the dish. Naturally regular grocery-store ingredients may be used and the dish will be good, but not as good as if only the very best were used. This dish may be assembled with a flourish at the table as Alfredo does in Rome, but the shyer type may prefer to do their concocting in the kitchen, and present the hot, gleaming, and golden dish in its finished state.

Menu: JAPANESE SOUP (see page 198)
      NOODLES ALFREDO
      SALAD: MIXED GREENS WITH GARLIC DRESSING (2 PARTS
          OLIVE OIL, 1 PART VINEGAR, ONE CLOVE GARLIC, SALT
          AND PEPPER. MIX THE DRESSING AND LET THE GARLIC
          STEEP AWHILE. REMOVE BEFORE ADDING TO THE
          GREENS.)
      LEMON SOUFFLÉ
      COFFEE

NOODLES ALFREDO:

1 pound the very best noodles, wide fettuccelle
or make your own according to recipe below
¾ cup freshly grated Parmesan cheese
½ cup very best unsalted butter

Cook the noodles in 3 quarts rapidly boiling water with 1 table-spoon salt. Cook 6 to 8 minutes until tender but still firm, what the Italians call *al dente,* which means it resists the tooth a bit when bitten. To make your own noodles, and they are well worth the little trouble, follow these simple directions:

2 cups flour
2 eggs, beaten lightly
½ teaspoon salt

Sprinkle the flour on a pastry board. Add the eggs and salt to the flour and mix well. Work with the fingers until the dough is stiff, satiny, and resilient. Cut the dough into 3 parts, roll each part out as thin as possible. Sprinkle the sheets of dough with a little flour and let dry a bit, about an hour, or until the noodles have turned a pale yellow color. Cut into strips ¾ inch wide. Put the drained, cooked noodles on a hot platter. Sprinkle some of the cheese and some of the butter over the noodles, spoon around and keep adding cheese and butter until the noodles are glistening with both. This should be done very rapidly. The heat of the noodles will melt the cheese and butter. Serves 4 generously, 6 modestly.

Swedish stuffed veal roast with sour cream gravy

TIME: 4½ HOURS

This not especially frugal or really everyday dish of another Swedish friend is so good it is included anyway.

Menu: SWEDISH STUFFED VEAL ROAST WITH SOUR CREAM GRAVY
BOILED POTATOES
RISOTTO (see page 138)
CHERRY TOMATOES
HOT DROP BISCUITS
RHUBARB BAKED WITH STRAWBERRIES
COFFEE

SWEDISH STUFFED VEAL ROAST
WITH SOUR CREAM GRAVY:

1 large onion, peeled and chopped
4 cups dried bread cubes or coarse crumbs
⅓ cup finely chopped parsley
1 teaspoon dry sage
Salt and pepper
¼ cup (½ stick) melted butter
1 roast, rolled and boned, of veal, either leg or breast (have the butcher leave a pocket for the dressing), around 6 pounds
5 or 6 slices bacon
Flour
Salt and pepper
1 pint sour cream

Mix the onion, bread cubes, parsley, sage, salt and pepper together and moisten with the melted butter. Put into the veal pocket, being careful not to pack too tightly, tie with string or skewer together with poultry pins. Place in a baking pan with the strips of bacon on top. Roast in a 300° oven, allowing 40 minutes per pound. If a meat thermometer is used the internal temperature should read 170° when done. Transfer the roast from pan to a hot platter and keep warm. Make a gravy by mixing 3 tablespoons of the juices in the pan with 3 tablespoons flour, blending until smooth. Add 1 cup water. This is served with boiled potatoes, and the Swedish use the water from the potatoes as the liquid in the gravy. Cook this a while until smooth and thick. Add salt and pepper and stir in the sour cream slowly, being careful not to let it boil. Serve with the roast. Serves 6 to 8 generously.

Charquicán (Chilean)

TIME: 1¼ HOURS

This is a Chilean stew, somewhat the consistency of baby food, that tastes better than it sounds. The Chilean who gave me the recipe says that it is the pumpkin that gives it the different and delicious flavor.

Menu: CHARQUICÁN
     GREEN PEPPER SALAD (see page 21)
     FRENCH BREAD
     ROQUEFORT CHEESE AND CRACKERS
     COFFEE

CHARQUICÁN:

1½ pounds top round (have the butcher cut in ½-inch slices, London-broil style)
3 tablespoons butter
1 cup string beans, cut very fine
1 cup peas
1 large pumpkin, cut in pieces
4 potatoes, boiled until very soft
Salt and pepper
¼ pound (1 stick) butter

Sauté the round-steak slices in the butter until browned on all sides. Remove from the fire and cut into ½-inch pieces (traditionally this cannot be done before it is sautéed). Put in a Dutch oven or heavy saucepan with the string beans, peas, pumpkin, potatoes, salt and pepper. Simmer slowly, stirring and mashing the potatoes. Most of the ingredients should be indistinguishable, though the meat and string beans and sometimes the peas keep their identity. Cut the butter up into pieces and stir it in until it is melted and well blended. Serve very hot. Serves 4.

Fave with spinach (Italian)

TIME: 12 TO 24 HOURS

Fave are the large, meaty Italian beans resembling a lima in shape but not in flavor, and are often called horse beans. The regular dried lima or kidney beans may be used interchangeably with them in this recipe and many others.

Menu: BAKED HAM SLICE
FAVE WITH SPINACH
GREEN PEPPER SALAD (see page 21)
HOT CORN BREAD
LEMON PUDDING
COFFEE

FAVE WITH SPINACH:
2 cloves garlic, minced
⅓ cup olive oil
2 pounds fresh spinach, well washed, shaken dry, and chopped, or 1 package frozen and chopped
1 pound fave or dried limas, soaked overnight and simmered until tender
Salt and pepper

Sauté the garlic in the olive oil until partly cooked. Add the spinach and stir around for 2 or 3 minutes. Add the cooked fave, limas, or kidney beans and heat together briefly for 10 to 15 minutes. Salt and pepper. Serves 6 to 8.

Matelote (French)

TIME: 1 HOUR

On all the seacoasts of the world various combinations of the good foods from the sea are cooked together. This is one of the daily ways the French cook them. It is simpler than a bouillabaisse, though not so well known, and can be made from just one variety of fish. It is customary to use carp and eel, but because the idea of cooking and eating eel is so upsetting to Americans it is omitted in this version.

Menu: MATELOTE
TOSSED GREEN SALAD WITH FRENCH DRESSING (3 PARTS OLIVE OIL, 1 PART VINEGAR, SALT AND PEPPER)
FRENCH BREAD
APPLE FRITTERS
COFFEE

MATELOTE:

   3 tablespoons butter
   1 large onion, chopped fine
   2 cloves garlic
   2 tablespoons chopped parsley
   1 bay leaf
   1 sprig fresh dill
   2 tablespoons chopped celery leaves
   2 cups red or white wine
   1 jigger brandy
   Dusting of spices (pinch nutmeg, ginger, cinnamon, pepper,
      very little salt)
   10 to 12 small onions, boiled, then browned in butter
   ½ pound small mushrooms, cooked in the same butter
   2 pounds fish, cut in thick slices, skin and all, usually
      some fresh-water fish such as carp, perch, or eel, but
      around the seacoast salt-water fish is used.

Sauté the onion and garlic in the butter, add the herbs and celery leaves, spices, and wine. Bring to a boil. Light the brandy and pour into the sauce. Simmer for about 30 minutes. Strain and put in another pan with the pieces of fish, the small onions, and the mushrooms. Simmer for about 10 minutes. Serve with croutons. Some people prefer to thicken the stew with 4 tablespoons butter mixed with 2 tablespoons flour, but with the preliminary cooking of the sauce it is not necessary. Serves 4 to 6.

Fried Japanese rice

TIME: 40 MINUTES

A Japanese artist gave me directions for this graceful way of using leftovers or preparing an unscheduled meal or for unexpected guests. She says this is only a basic plan that may be varied indefinitely according to taste and what's in the larder.

Menu: FRIED JAPANESE RICE
COLD CHERRY TOMATOES
FRESH, WARM GINGERBREAD
TEA

FRIED JAPANESE RICE:

> *3 strips bacon, diced*
> *1 large onion, chopped fine*
> *⅓ cup finely chopped parsley*
> *⅓ cup coarsely chopped celery*
> *1 cup diced cooked meat, preferably chicken, pork, or beef*
> *2 cups cooked rice (leftover rice may be used)*
> *Soy sauce*
> *Salt and pepper*
> *2 whole eggs*

Sauté the bacon and pour off most of the fat. Leave a thick film covering the bottom of the skillet, add the onion, parsley, and celery. Stir around until the onion and celery are pale yellow and partly cooked but still crisp. Add the meat and rice. Season with soy sauce, salt and pepper, heat briefly, break the eggs onto the mixture and scramble over low heat until the eggs are cooked. Serves 4.

Potato omelet (tortilla de patatas—Spanish)

TIME: 50 MINUTES

Gastronomy knowing no exact boundaries, this is much like a simpler version of the French *omelette Parmentier*. The proportions vary according to the number of people and your whim. In Spain there is usually a meat course served with this meal.

Menu: GAZPACHO (see page 30)
      TORTILLA DE PATATAS
      FRENCH BREAD
      FRESH PLUMS AND CREAM CHEESE
      COFFEE

TORTILLA DE PATATAS:
    ⅓ cup olive oil
    2 medium-sized potatoes, peeled and cubed
    4 eggs, beaten
    Salt

Sauté the potatoes in the oil, turning frequently until cooked but not browned. Remove from the oil, drain, and let cool until lukewarm. Drain off the surplus fat in the skillet, leaving just a film on the bottom. Reheat the skillet. Mix the beaten eggs, salt, and potatoes. Pour into the hot skillet, lifting the edges frequently until the omelet is browned on the bottom. Turn on the other side with a spatula and brown. It may even be scrambled slightly if that is easier. Serves 4.

Swedish brown beans

TIME: 12 HOURS; 24 HOURS IF SOAKED OVERNIGHT

Swedish brown beans are a little like Mexican pink beans in appearance, but are cooked very simply with a sweet and sour sauce. Sometimes it is made with butter, sugar, and vinegar slightly thickened with flour, other times with molasses in place of the sugar, as in this version, and no thickening. The beans are always served with either Swedish meat balls or fried pork.

Menu: KÖTTBULLAR (see page 124)
   SWEDISH BROWN BEANS
   PRESSED CUCUMBER SALAD (see menu, page 168)
   SWEDISH CRISP BREAD
   BAKED RHUBARB
   COFFEE

SWEDISH BROWN BEANS:
  2 cups Swedish-style brown beans (get at Scandinavian food stores)
  1 tablespoon salt
  3 tablespoons vinegar
  3 tablespoons molasses
  Freshly grated nutmeg

Soak the beans overnight, drain, cover with fresh water, and simmer until barely tender. Drain, add salt, vinegar, molasses, and nutmeg. Swish the beans around, heat together briefly and serve. Serves 6 generously.

Veal and pork goulash with sauerkraut (székely goulyas—Czechoslovakian)

TIME: 2 HOURS

Once an American has eaten some of the good European dishes lovingly assembled with sauerkraut, he loses his prejudices. It's all in knowing how to cook it and taking the time and care. This dish, properly made, is a very delicate one.

Menu: SZÉKELY GOULYAS
    HOT FRENCH BREAD (BROWN-AND-SERVE KIND)
    SALAD: TOSSED GREENS WITH SLICED AVOCADO AND THIN
        RINGS OF RAW ONION WITH A FRENCH DRESSING (2
        PARTS OLIVE OIL, 1 PART VINEGAR, SALT AND PEPPER)
    GINGERBREAD
    COFFEE

SZÉKELY GOULYAS:
> 2 tablespoons fat
> 1 pound veal, cut into stew-sized pieces
> 1 pound pork, cut into stew-sized pieces
> 2 pounds bulk sauerkraut or two large cans
> 2 tablespoons caraway seeds
> 1 pint sour cream
> Salt and pepper

Melt the fat and sauté the veal and pork until brown on all sides. Put in a Dutch oven or deep pot. Rinse the sauerkraut with fresh water and squeeze out the excess liquid with your hands if you like the sauerkraut mild, otherwise just drain it. Put in the pot with the meat, add the caraway seeds, cover tightly, and cook over a low flame about 1½ hours. About 10 or 15 minutes before serving add the sour cream, salt and pepper, blending in smoothly. Serves 4.

Pizza (Italian)

TIME: 1½ HOURS

Aside from spaghetti with meat sauce probably the best-beloved and best-known of Italian dishes served in this country is pizza. It is often redundantly called pizza pie though *pizza* is the Italian word for pie. Italians who are purists say that it cannot be baked in home ovens because it is impossible to get them as hot as the commercial ones. Obviously in this recipe I am going along with the impurists.

Menu: PIZZA

> TOSSED SALAD WITH FRENCH DRESSING (2 PARTS OLIVE OIL, 1 PART VINEGAR, SALT AND PEPPER)
>
> FRESH PEACHES IN RED WINE
>
> COFFEE

Pizza Dough:

> 1 package dry yeast
> 2 tablespoons lukewarm water
> 1½ teaspoons sugar
> 2½ teaspoons salt
> ½ cup shortening
> 2 cups boiling water
> 6 cups or more sifted flour

Topping:

> ¼ cup olive oil
> 1 clove garlic, cut in half, soaked in the olive oil
> 1 large can Italian plum tomatoes, drained
> 1 cup grated Parmesan cheese
> Salt and pepper
> 1 lump Mozzarella cheese, coarsely shredded or thinly sliced
> Orégano
> (For variation use 2 or 3 small cans of anchovies cut into pieces instead of the Mozzarella)

Soften the yeast in the lukewarm water. Blend the sugar, salt, and shortening in a bowl. Add the boiling water and stir until the shortening is melted. Cool to lukewarm and add the yeast mixture, stirring well. Add about half the sifted flour and beat thoroughly. Gradually add the remaining flour. Divide the dough into 4 portions and turn onto a lightly floured board. Roll out immediately into 4 rounds about 12 inches in diameter and about ¼ inch thick. Put on a greased cooky sheet and let rise in a warm place until double in bulk. When the rounds have risen, brush with the olive oil and cover the dough with the drained tomatoes, sprinkle with the grated Parmesan cheese, and then with the salt and pepper. Arrange or strew the Mozzarella cheese generously over the pies. Sprinkle this lightly with the orégano. Bake in a 450° or 500° oven for 20 minutes. Serve very hot in wedges or give each person a whole pie. Serves 4 generously, a pie to each.

Greek pilaf with sautéed kidneys

TIME: 50 MINUTES

This pilaf is presented somewhat the same as a curry or a *rijsttafel* with small bowls of accompaniments to sprinkle on.

Menu: COLD CUCUMBER SOUP (BLEND 2 MASHED CLOVES GARLIC
WITH 5 TABLESPOONS OLIVE OIL; MIX 1 LARGE CUCUM-
BER PEELED AND DICED WITH 1 PINT SOUR CREAM AND 6
ICE CUBES UNTIL THICK AND COLD; MIX WITH A ROTARY
BEATER UNTIL SUFFICIENTLY THICK TO DISCARD THE
ICE CUBES; OR IN AN ELECTRIC BLENDER, AND CRACK
THE ICE BEFORE PUTTING IN THE BLENDER.)
GREEK PILAF WITH SAUTÉED KIDNEYS
FRENCH BREAD
PEACHES IN RED WINE
COFFEE

GREEK PILAF WITH SAUTÉED KIDNEYS:

6 lamb kidneys, split and white part cut out
⅓ cup olive oil
1 cup uncooked rice
2 cups beef bouillon or chicken broth
Juice of ½ lemon
Salt and pepper
Small bowl crumbled cooked bacon, sliced raw onion,
  water cress, chopped red pepper

Sauté the kidneys briefly in the olive oil. Remove and keep warm. Add the rice and cook over a low flame, stirring until well coated and pale yellow. Add the bouillon, or broth, and lemon juice, salt and pepper, bearing in mind that the bouillon and broth are seasoned. Cover and simmer over a low flame for 14 minutes. Remove cover and fluff the rice with a fork. Put the warm kidneys on top and serve with the accompaniments described above. Serves 4.

Belgian tomato salad

TIME: 5 TO 6 HOURS

According to an old Belgian cookbook, tomatoes sliced in a dish with a little vinegar and olive oil is ignorance—not a salad. But with care it can be sublime.

Menu: CANADIAN BACON, COOKED IN ONE PIECE
NOODLES ALFREDO (see page 82)
BELGIAN TOMATO SALAD
BLACK WALNUT PIE
COFFEE

BELGIAN TOMATO SALAD:
6 *medium-sized tomatoes, preferably 3 red and 3 yellow ones*
1 *onion, peeled and sliced*
Salt
1 *teaspoon sugar*

Dressing:
½ *teaspoon salt*
1 *teaspoon tarragon vinegar*
2 *teaspoons olive oil*
Pinch dry mustard
Pepper
1 *teaspoon chopped chervil*

Plunge the tomatoes into boiling water, remove immediately and skin, being careful not to puncture the flesh and let the juice out. Put the slices of onion in the bottom of a salad dish and arrange the tomato slices over them. Sprinkle with salt and sugar. In 4 hours lift the tomatoes and remove the onions. Put in another salad dish. Mix the ingredients for the dressing, adding the oil very slowly. Pour over the tomatoes and marinate for at least 1 hour before serving. Serves 4.

Whitebait (French and Italian)

TIME: 45 MINUTES TO 1 HOUR

All over the world gourmets and the plain people eat the best and the most varied food. Those in between, beset with many prejudices, miss many good things from the land and from the sea. These tiny inch-long fish, of suitable proportions for a doll's aquarium, are almost ambrosial. They are floured and fried whole in deep fat. You will find them on the seacoast in the very best of restaurants and in the simplest; nowhere else.

Menu: WHITEBAIT WITH LEMON WEDGES
THIN STALKS OF BELGIAN ENDIVE WITH SEASONED OLIVE
    OIL TO DIP THEM IN
FRENCH BREAD AND SWEET BUTTER
FRESH STRAWBERRIES IN THE HULL SURROUNDING A
    MOUND OF POWDERED SUGAR
COFFEE

WHITEBAIT:

2 pounds whitebait
Flour
Salt and pepper
Fat for deep frying
Lemon wedges

Dust the whitebait with flour seasoned with salt and pepper, and fry a few at a time in deep fat heated to 345° to 355° until brown and crisp. Drain on a paper towel and serve with wedges of lemon. These must be fried a few at a time or they form a sticky mass. Serves 4.

Gratin de pomme de terre à la Dauphinoise (potatoes baked with cheese and milk—French)

TIME: 1½ HOURS

It is a constant surprise and delight to find how many ways other countries have of cooking a simple vegetable in a simple but imaginative way and presenting it importantly.

Menu: COLD HAM, PREFERABLY GOOD VIRGINIA HAM
GRATIN DE POMME DE TERRE À LA DAUPHINOISE
ROUMANIAN GREEN PEPPER SALAD (see page 21)
MERINGUE SHELLS FILLED WITH BRANDIED BLACK BING
CHERRIES
COFFEE

GRATIN DE POMME DE TERRE À LA DAUPHINOISE:
2 pounds Idaho potatoes, peeled and grated
Salt
Black pepper, freshly ground
½ teaspoon grated nutmeg
1 egg, beaten with
3 cups milk
¼ pound grated Switzerland Swiss cheese
1 clove garlic, cut in half
More grated Switzerland Swiss cheese
3 tablespoons unsalted butter

Mix the potatoes with salt, pepper, nutmeg, egg and milk mixture, and the grated cheese. Butter a casserole and rub well with the cut pieces of garlic. Spoon in the potato mixture. Sprinkle the top lavishly with more of the grated cheese and dot with lumps of butter. Cook in a medium oven 40 to 45 minutes. Serve piping hot. Serves 4 to 6.

Vegetable dolma (Armenian)

TIME: 1 HOUR, 20 MINUTES

The Armenians are more untrammeled and colorful than we are when they stuff vegetables. Sure, they stuff green peppers, but for the same meal they stuff zucchini or yellow squash, small eggplants, and tomatoes. Arranged on a platter, they are very pretty. The same filling is used for all, but each vegetable flavors it differently.

Menu: VEGETABLE DOLMAS

    PIDEH, THE ARMENIAN BREAD, OR FRENCH BREAD

    A RICH DESSERT, BAKLAAVA, STRUDEL, OR A LARGE LAYER
      CAKE

    COFFEE

VEGETABLE DOLMA:

3 green peppers
3 large, firm tomatoes
3 medium-sized zucchini
3 eggplants
1½ pounds shoulder lamb, ground
1½ cups uncooked rice
3 onions, chopped
3 tablespoons chopped parsley
1 teaspoon chopped fresh mint leaves
Salt and pepper

Wash the vegetables. Cut the tops off the peppers, scrape out the seeds and the white parts. Drain the seeds from the tomatoes. Scoop out good-sized hollows in the eggplants and zucchini, leaving a shell about ½ to ¾ inch thick. Mix the meat with the rice, onion, parsley, mint, salt and pepper. Fill the vegetables with the mixture, being careful not to fill too full or pack. Arrange the vegetables in a shallow casserole, with about ½ inch of water in the dish. Cover and bake in 350° oven or over low heat until tender, which should be 30 to 40 minutes. Arrange decoratively on plain-colored earthenware dish that will be a good background for the brightly colored vegetables. This serves 4 generously, though not all 4 can have the same combination of vegetables.

Veal Paprika (Hungarian)

TIME: 1¾ HOURS

Basically Hungarian paprika is just a stew with some sour cream and paprika added, but somehow these two simple touches seem to take it out of the routine class and make it into a dish to please and honor the most finicky guests.

Menu: VEAL PAPRIKA
   SPAETZLE (see page 103)
   SWEET AND SOUR GREEN BEANS (see menu, page 132)
   HOT ROLLS
   FRESH BLUEBERRY TART
   COFFEE

VEAL PAPRIKA:

   3 tablespoons butter
   2 cloves garlic, minced
   2 onions, sliced thin
   1½ pounds veal steak, cut up for stew
   1 tablespoon Italian tomato paste
   2 tablespoons Hungarian paprika
   Salt
   1 cup sour cream

Sauté the garlic and the onion in the butter until pale yellow. Add the pieces of veal and sauté until a light brown. Add 1½ cups water and the tomato paste and simmer for 1 hour or more until tender. Remove from the fire and add the paprika, salt, and sour cream. Heat together, but do not let cook. Serves 4.

Spaetzle

TIME: 40 MINUTES

Spaetzle, sometimes translated as pinched-off noodles, is traditional and delicious with chicken or veal paprika, or served in a casserole with butter and grated cheese.

Menu: MITITEI (see page 80)
SPAETZLE, WITH BUTTER AND CHEESE
BELGIAN TOMATO SALAD (see page 98)
HOT POPPY-SEED ROLLS
RHUBARB PIE
COFFEE

SPAETZLE:

3 eggs, slightly beaten
1 cup flour, measured after sifting
Salt
Toss with:
2 or 3 tablespoons butter
⅓ cup grated cheese, Parmesan or Swiss

Mix the eggs, flour, and salt together until smooth. Put the dough on a wet breadboard and pat out thin. Take a wet knife and cut into 1-inch-wide strips with the dull side of the knife. Cut or pinch off 1-inch pieces of these strips and drop into a pan of boiling salted water. They are done when they come to the top. Serve with veal or chicken paprika or put into a hot casserole. Add 2 or 3 tablespoons sweet butter and about ⅓ cup grated cheese, either Switzerland Swiss cheese or Parmesan, and toss together and serve. Serves 4.

Austrian pot cheese dumplings

TIME: 1 HOUR

These are somewhat like the Roumanian but made just a little differently and presented a little differently. They are often served with a sweet sauce following the salad for lunch.

Menu: FRENCH BOILED-BEEF SALAD (see page 51)
FRENCH BREAD
AUSTRIAN POT CHEESE DUMPLINGS
COFFEE

AUSTRIAN POT CHEESE DUMPLINGS:
1 pound pot cheese
3 eggs
1 cup bread crumbs or matzoh meal
½ teaspoon baking powder
1 tablespoon sugar
Pinch of salt
Flour

Sauce:
1 stick butter (½ cup), melted
¼ cup sugar (brown tastes particularly good)
1 teaspoon powdered cinnamon

Push the pot cheese through a sieve, add the three unbeaten eggs, the bread crumbs or matzoh meal, baking powder, sugar, and salt. Mix thoroughly and add enough flour to make a medium-soft dumpling. Roll and pat dumplings into the size of an egg. Drop into salted boiling water. Cover and cook for about half an hour. Make a sauce by mixing the melted butter with the sugar and cinnamon, cooking for a minute or two. Serve in a bowl to be spooned over the hot, drained dumplings. Serves 4.

Himmel und erde (North German vegetable dish)

TIME: 1 HOUR

This is a North German country dish, meaning heaven and earth, that is eaten almost endlessly by those who like it. It can be made from the cooked vegetables in the refrigerator. They eat it alone and blissfully, but this menu might suit American eating habits more.

Menu: BROILED PORK CHOPS
HIMMEL UND ERDE
SALTY RYE
CHEESECAKE
COFFEE

HIMMEL UND ERDE:

2 cups applesauce (Heaven)
1 pound potatoes or turnips (Earth), cooked and mashed
1 pound finely slivered green beans, cooked
2 medium-sized onions, sliced and sautéed in butter
4 to 6 slices bacon, cooked and crumbled

Serve the cold applesauce, hot potatoes or turnips, and hot green beans together on a plate and top with the sautéed onions and crumbled bacon (in Germany blood sausage is traditional).

Persian shish kebab

TIME: 5 TO 6 HOURS MARINATING TIME
TIME: 10 TO 15 MINUTES BROILING

Davoud Yonan, the Persian friend who made this wonderfully aromatic dish for me, puts certain difficulties in the way of those who try to duplicate this exactly. His mother gets the tarragon seeds from her family in Iran and his sister grows it. The Persian tarragon tastes much like ours, though the shape of the leaf is very different and the flavor slightly so. The orégano obtained in the same roundabout way is more like ours. Though delicious, brandy seemed a little odd to me, but he said that it was always used. His mother still cooks the food the way they did in Persia when she left about thirty-five years ago. The Persians being nomads for centuries, Davoud skewered this and broiled it skewer by skewer over the flame of the gas stove, protesting that it is much, much better over an open fire. It tasted very good this way, but took longer than in a broiler and there was a tendency for the food to cool, as presumably it does in the open.

Menu: PERSIAN SHISH KEBAB
ARMENIAN PILAF (see page 108)
ROUMANIAN CUCUMBER SALAD (see page 159)
PEACHES IN RED WINE
COFFEE

PERSIAN SHISH KEBAB:

> 2 pounds lamb, cut from the leg by the butcher and cut into 2-inch squares (also it should be very young lamb from an Armenian butcher who understands the importance of such things)
> 2 tablespoons lemon juice
> ⅓ cup olive oil
> 1 large onion, sliced thin
> 1 tablespoon chopped fresh tarragon or 1 teaspoon dried
> 1 teaspoon chopped fresh orégano or ½ teaspoon dried
> 1 jigger brandy
> Salt and pepper
> 1 pound fresh mushrooms, caps only
> 1 pound small fresh tomatoes, cut in quarters

Put the pieces of lamb in a large bowl. Mix the lemon juice, olive oil, onion, tarragon, orégano, brandy, salt and pepper and pour over the meat. Put in the refrigerator overnight. Turn the pieces of lamb from time to time and stir around so all the pieces become well marinated. Before cooking remove the bowl from the refrigerator and let come to room temperature. This will take about 1 hour. Take the skewers (the long ones available in Armenian food stores are best), put a piece of the meat on, a piece of mushroom, a quarter of tomato, and repeat until all the skewers are loaded loosely. Broil one at a time over an open fire, indoors or out, or on top of the stove, and, of course, it *can* be done in a broiler. The mushrooms and the tomatoes should be browned and blistered, but should still be slightly raw. Serves 4 generously.

Armenian pilaf

TIME: 45 MINUTES

An Armenian friend of mine who likes to entertain often and well, but does not like to cook, serves this meal, which may be prepared ahead with little last-minute fussing. Even the pilaf, cooked with this amount of butter, may be done 2 or 3 hours ahead and reheated when needed.

Menu: COLD STUFFED GRAPE LEAVES CHILLED IN LEMON JUICE
(MAY BE BOUGHT CANNED AND STUFFED AT ANY ARME-
NIAN STORE)
SHISH KEBAB
PILAF
TOSSED GREEN SALAD WITH FRENCH DRESSING (2 PARTS
OLIVE OIL, 1 PART VINEGAR, SALT AND PEPPER)
RUM CAKE
COFFEE

PILAF:
¼ pound butter
1 cup uncooked rice
1 large onion, chopped (often omitted)
2 cups chicken broth
Salt and pepper if necessary

Melt the butter in a heavy saucepan and add the uncooked rice and onion, if used. Stir around until the rice is coated and pale yellow. Add the chicken broth and additional seasoning if necessary. Cover and cook 20 to 25 minutes or until the rice is tender. The Armenians then remove the cover and put a clean napkin over the top of the pot to absorb any moisture, then cover again. To reheat, stir a bit over a low fire. It seldom needs any more liquid because this much butter keeps it moist. Serves 4.

Blini with sour cream and red caviar (Russian)

TIME: 1½ HOURS

Only Americans are so dull as to serve pancakes only as a break-fast dish. In Europe they are a main dish, a dessert, an everyday dish, a party dish. Blini, the Russian version, is just plain heavenly with melted butter, sour cream, and caviar as a main dish. In Russia the black caviar is often used, but here it is easier to be lavish with the red, or salmon, caviar, and also more colorful.

Menu: BLINI, WITH MELTED BUTTER, SOUR CREAM, AND RED
     CAVIAR
     SALAD: TOMATO ASPIC WITH GREENS AND MAYONNAISE
     FRUIT
     COFFEE

BLINI:
   A good buckwheat pancake mix may be used, or this version:
1 cup sifted flour
1 teaspoon baking powder
1 teaspoon sugar
1½ cups milk
2 tablespoons sour cream
2 eggs
Butter for frying

Sift the flour and baking powder together. Add sugar, then the milk and sour cream. Stir until smooth. Add the eggs beaten until frothy, mix, and let stand for about ½ hour. Heat the butter in a skillet. When a few drops of water dance when flicked on the skillet, fry the pancakes, making them about 3 inches in diameter. Drain on paper before serving. Serve with a small pitcher of melted butter, a bowl of sour cream (the kind you buy), and a bowl of red caviar. Serves 4.

Eggs ranch-style (huevos rancheros—Mexican)

TIME: 40 MINUTES

Most Mexicans and New Mexicans cook eggs this way. It is a very hot version of a *piperade* (see page 34). The chile *tepines* are hot little berries that look much like juniper berries and burn your mouth if you bite into one raw. If chile tepines are not available, a couple of red chile pods, or hot chile powder, will do.

Menu: HUEVOS RANCHEROS
FRENCH-FRIED POTATOES
FRENCH BREAD
LIME SHERBET SPRINKLED WITH CHOCOLATE BITS
COFFEE

HUEVOS RANCHEROS:
2 *tablespoons olive oil*
2 *cloves garlic, minced*
1 *small onion, minced*
1 *teaspoon orégano*
6 *medium-sized fresh tomatoes, chopped*
2 *chile tepines, or 4 green chile pods chopped, either canned or fresh, or 4 tablespoons powdered red chile*
Salt and pepper
8 *eggs*

Sauté the garlic and onion in the olive oil, add the orégano, tomatoes, chile tepines, salt and pepper. Simmer together over a low flame until thick and mushy. Break the eggs into the mixture and let them poach until the white is cooked. Serve in the sauce with plenty of French bread and good cold beer to mitigate the fieriness of this dish. Serves 4.

Spaghettini (Italian)

This wonderfully simple, wonderfully good version of pasta is sometimes baked in a pie tin, then served in wedges either hot or cold. It is often made at Easter time.

Menu: CANADIAN BACON, COOKED UNTIL FRIZZLED
SPAGHETTINI
COOKED GREEN BEANS, MARINATED IN FRENCH DRESSING
(2 PARTS OLIVE OIL, 1 PART VINEGAR, SALT AND PEP-
PER) AND SPRINKLED WITH CHOPPED BLACK WALNUTS
KEY WEST LIME PIE
COFFEE

SPAGHETTINI:

1 pound spaghetti or spaghettini (the finer version)
2 or 3 eggs, beaten
½ cup freshly grated Parmesan cheese
Salt and lots of black pepper, preferably freshly ground

Cook the spaghetti in rapidly boiling salted water in a large pan until tender but not mushy. Drain quickly and mix with the beaten eggs and cheese with a large fork and spoon the way one mixes a salad, until all the strands are coated and glistening. Transfer to a buttered pie tin, packing slightly, and bake in a medium oven 15 to 20 minutes, or serve as it is. Serves 4.

Cassoulet Toulousain (French)

TIME: 4 HOURS

If Tiffany or Hollywood were baking beans they might do just such a dish as this. Tiffany would do one as elegant and Hollywood would make such a production. Certainly it is the most impressive, expensive, and labor-consuming of all bean dishes. There are those who think, and with some reason, that a cassoulet can only be made with some pieces of goose and goose fat to give it that inimitable flavor. Certainly the goose fat adds to the beans a flavor as special as that of pork. However, Marcel Perret, of the Café St. Denis in New York, a chef with integrity and no compromise, gave me this recipe for the cassoulet that he serves weekly in his restaurant. When he gave me this recipe, he said, more realistically than he sometimes does, that Americans just did not have parts of goose around handy. However, in many speciality food stores goose fat may be bought.

Menu: CASSOULET TOULOUSAIN
       TOSSED GREEN SALAD WITH FRENCH DRESSING (2 PARTS
          OLIVE OIL, 1 PART WINE VINEGAR, SALT AND PEPPER)
       FRENCH BREAD
       STRAWBERRIES, SLIGHTLY SWEETENED AND CHILLED IN
          RED WINE
       COFFEE

CASSOULET TOULOUSAIN:

2 pounds navy beans
2 cloves garlic
2 carrots, cut in pieces
2 onions, with cloves imbedded
Bouquet garni (celery leaves, thyme, bay leaf)
Pieces of fresh pork rind
Salt
½ pound lean salt pork
1 pound garlic sausage
1 pound boneless lamb, leg or shoulder
3 medium-sized onions, chopped
3 cloves garlic, minced fine
3 tablespoons tomato paste
1 roasted duck (or pieces of goose if you're being authentic) removed from bones and cut in bite-size pieces
Gravy fat and juices from the roasted duck
Salt and pepper
Bread crumbs

Cook the beans in water to cover with garlic, carrot, onions and clove, bouquet garni, pork rinds, and salt for 1 hour. Scald the salt pork and sausage and add to the beans. Cook until tender. Brown the lamb and add to the lamb the chopped onion, garlic, and tomato paste and some of the liquid that the beans have been cooked in. Simmer for a few minutes together. Remove pork rind and bouquet garni. Use a deep bean pot (or better yet the French pot made from *issel* clay that takes its name from this dish). Into the cassoulet put a layer each of the beans, slices of salt pork, sausage, lamb mixture, duck, and repeat until all the ingredients are used. Add the duck gravy and season. Top with some fine bread crumbs. Bake in the oven 30 to 45 minutes to mellow the flavors and serve very hot. Serves 8 to 10.

Cheese soup (Swiss)

TIME: 1 HOUR

In Switzerland when the skiers come down from the mountains they are often given bowls of hot, steaming cheese soup that seems ample and satisfying for even these hungry people. Naturally others eat it too.

Menu: CHEESE SOUP
ARTICHOKES WITH ONION AND DILL (see page 49)
FRENCH BREAD
CHERRY TART
COFFEE

CHEESE SOUP:

1 large Bermuda onion, chopped fine
2 tablespoons butter
2 tablespoons flour
1 cup beef stock or bouillon
2 cups milk
1 cup freshly grated cheese, Switzerland Swiss or a good Cheddar

Sauté the onion in the butter until pale yellow and tender. Sprinkle with the flour and stir until it is well blended with the butter and onion. Add the bouillon slowly and cook until smooth and thick. Add the milk and simmer, but do not boil. After about 15 minutes remove from the fire and stir in the cheese, letting it melt in the soup. Stir until smooth and serve immediately. Serves 4 people or 2 skiers.

Pissaladiera (French Provençal)

TIME: 1½ HOURS

In Provence in the South of France near the Italian border they make a dish called *pissaladiera* that is a lusty French variant of pizza. Most versions do not have tomatoes, but here and there you will find someone who adds them in the Italian fashion.

Menu: PISSALADIERA
       BELGIAN TOMATO SALAD (see page 98)
       HOT ROLLS
       COFFEE

PISSALADIERA:

2 large or 3 medium-sized onions, peeled and sliced
1 fat clove garlic, minced
¼ cup olive oil
Salt and pepper
Bay leaf
Bread dough (see pizza recipe, page 94), *or use hot-roll mix*
⅔ cup black olives, the kind that comes in tubs in foreign groceries, and are used unpitted
1 tin French rolled anchovies

Sauté the onion and garlic in the hot oil and add the salt and pepper and bay leaf. Cook until the onions are a light, even brown, and remove the bay leaf. Line a 9-inch pie pan with the bread dough. Spread the onion, garlic, and oil mixture over the bottom of the dough. Rinse the olives, drain well, and strew over the onions. Arrange the anchovies here and there. Bake in a 450° to 500° oven for about 15 minutes or until brown. Serve cut in strips or wedges. For the main meal or for hungry people double the quantity. Serves 4 for a light meal.

Fish pudding (fiskebudding—Norwegian)

TIME: 1½ HOURS, MAKING SAUCE WHILE PUDDING IS IN OVEN

Most of Norway lives on sea food economically and enthusiastically. They make fine fish puddings with a shrimp or lobster sauce, each cook making it a little differently from the next though using practically the same ingredients.

Menu: FISKEBUDDING
      FRENCH-FRIED HEARTS OF ARTICHOKE
      NEW POTATOES, BOILED IN THEIR JACKETS
      KISSEL
      COFFEE

FISKEBUDDING:

3 pounds fresh cod or haddock fillets
2 tablespoons cornstarch, or, more traditionally, potato flour
Pinch grated nutmeg
1 tablespoon salt
1½ cups cream
Milk if necessary

Put the fillets through the meat grinder 4 times, at least, using the finest blade. Mix with the cornstarch, or potato flour, nutmeg, and salt. Add the cream and mix thoroughly. It should be about as thick as mashed potatoes. If necessary add a little more milk. Turn into a buttered mold and set in a shallow pan of water. Bake in a 350° oven about 1 hour. Turn out on a platter and serve with shrimp or lobster sauce.

Shrimp or lobster sauce:

> 2 tablespoons butter
> 2 tablespoons flour
> 1⅓ cups milk
> 1 cup cooked and cleaned shrimp, or diced, cooked lobster
> Salt
> Sherry

Melt the butter, add the flour, and cook for 2 or 3 minutes, until well blended. Add the milk slowly, stirring all the while until smooth and thick. Add the sherry and stir. Last, add the shrimp or lobster. Serves 4 to 6.

Baked lamb with boulgour (kibbe—Syrian)

TIME: 2 HOURS, INCLUDING CHILLING TIME

This is a traditional way of cooking and serving *boulgour,* the cracked ground wheat with the nutlike texture and flavor that is so delicious.

Menu: KIBBE
RICE
ROUMANIAN CUCUMBER SALAD (see page 159)
FRENCH OR ARMENIAN BREAD
FRESH PEARS
COFFEE

KIBBE:

1 cup boulgour, medium grind
1 pound lean lamb, put through the grinder twice
2 medium-sized onions, chopped
¼ pound (1 stick) butter
¼ cup pine nuts or pignolias
⅓ cup finely chopped parsley
1 pound lamb, with fat, put through the grinder once
Salt and pepper

Soak the wheat in cold water, drain, and press the excess water out. Chill in the refrigerator for about 1 hour to make it easier to handle. Mix the finely ground lamb with half the chopped onions and grind together. Sauté the remaining onions until a golden yellow. Mix with the pine nuts, and then with the meat mixture. Stir around in the pan a minute or two and let cool. Mix the boulgour with the other lamb and fat, salt and pepper, and knead a minute or two with the hands to mix thoroughly. Divide into two parts, putting one part on the bottom of a square 9- or 10-inch casserole that has been well buttered. Pat smooth and spread the meat mixture on top. Cover with the rest of the boulgour, patting down smoothly. Cut cater-corner into diamond shapes about 2½ to 3 inches on the sides. Bake in 375° oven about 1 hour, or until the top is brown and crusty. Serve diamond-shaped pieces on each plate with a spoonful of rice. Serves 4.

Roumanian potatoes (iahnie de carotofie)

TIME: 1 HOUR

Mashed potatoes, fried potatoes, baked and boiled potatoes are all good, but so are these, and a nice fresh approach to an almost daily dish.

Menu: BROILED LOIN LAMB CHOPS WITH KIDNEYS (HAVE THE BUTCHER LEAVE THE KIDNEYS IN)

IAHNIE DE CAROTOFIE

GARDEN LETTUCE WITH A DRESSING OF HEAVY CREAM (¼ CUP HEAVY CREAM, 1½ TEASPOONS FRESH LEMON JUICE, AND 1 TEASPOON GRATED LEMON PEEL)

HONEYDEW MELON SPRINKLED WITH FRESH LIME JUICE

COFFEE

IAHNIE DE CAROTOFIE:

1 large onion, chopped fine
¼ cup olive oil
4 to 6 large potatoes, peeled and cut in lengthwise quarters
1 cup bouillon
1 tomato, chopped with seeds removed, or 2 tablespoons Italian tomato paste
1 tablespoon finely chopped fresh dill
Salt and pepper if needed (the bouillon has some, so check carefully)

Sauté the onion in the oil until pale yellow and soft. Add the potatoes and bouillon and simmer until tender but not mushy. Add the tomato or tomato paste, dill, salt and pepper if necessary. Simmer for a few minutes. Let cool somewhat before serving. As with many Roumanian vegetable dishes, the flavors taste better if not served at stove heat. Often it is served at room temperature. Serves 4 to 6.

Empanados (Chilean)

TIME: 1¼ HOURS

These are the meat pies of South America, much like the Cornish pasties, and, like them, eaten hot or lukewarm.

Menu: EMPANADOS
   SALADE NIÇOISE (see page 70)
   HOT POPPY-SEED ROLLS
   FRESH PINEAPPLE CHUNKS WITH RASPBERRIES
   COFFEE

EMPANADOS:

3 medium-sized onions, chopped fine
2 tablespoons fat
1 pound round steak, ground, or leftover chopped meat, either beef or lamb
½ cup stock
½ cup seedless raisins
1 teaspoon cumin seed (comino)
1 teaspoon orégano
About 20 olives, green, stuffed or plain, or ripe, or one small can chopped ripe olives, drained
Salt and red pepper
2 hard-cooked eggs, sliced thin
1 recipe pie dough, or pie-crust mix

Sauté the onions in the fat until pale yellow and partly tender. Add the round steak and sauté that awhile, stirring so every part is browned. Add the stock, seedless raisins, cumin seed, orégano, and olives. Simmer for about 30 minutes. Add the salt and pepper, add the sliced hard-cooked eggs, and let cool. This is important. When the mixture is too hot it melts the pie dough. Roll the pie dough out rather thick, say about ⅓ inch, and cut in rounds about the size of a saucer. Put 2 tablespoons of the cooled meat on each round, pinch together, and bake in a 375° to 400° oven 20 to 25 minutes or until the empanados are well browned. Serves 4 to 6.

Another version of this dish is called *pastel choclo*. The same meat mixture is used, but in this dish it is placed in the bottom of a casserole and a can of cream-style corn mixed with 2 beaten eggs, 2 tablespoons sugar, a dash of flour, salt and pepper is poured over the meat. Put in a medium oven for ½ to ¾ hour until nicely browned. Serves 4.

Chinese ham and mustard green soup

TIME: 30 MINUTES

It always seems incredible to me that the clear and pretty Chinese or Japanese soups, with their meager ingredients, could have any flavor, but they do—and each a very delicate one. This one is particularly decorative, with the pink ham and the bright greens. Chinese ham has much the same flavor and texture as our Virginia ham, which is admittedly expensive. Naturally a less expensive one, more widely available, could be used.

Menu: CHINESE HAM AND MUSTARD GREEN SOUP
TÍO PEPE (see page 22)
SALADE NIÇOISE (see page 70)
HOT CORN BREAD
LEMON PUDDING
COFFEE

CHINESE HAM AND MUSTARD GREEN SOUP:

1 quart chicken broth or beef bouillon or even water
¼ pound Virginia ham, cut in thin pieces 1½ by 2 inches long
2 or 3 pieces ginger root, or ½ teaspoon ground ginger
Salt
½ pound mustard greens, cut in 1½-inch pieces

Simmer the ham in the broth, stock, or water with the ginger and salt for about 15 minutes. Remove the ham, add the mustard greens, do not cover. Bring to a boil, stir, add the ham, and serve. Serves 4.

French lentils with bacon

TIME: 3 HOURS

The French cook lentils often, like this, in soups, or for cold hors d'oeuvre.

Menu: FRENCH LENTILS WITH BACON
TOSSED GREEN SALAD WITH FRENCH DRESSING, ANY VARIATION
GARLIC BREAD
STRAWBERRIES IN RED WINE
COFFEE

FRENCH LENTILS WITH BACON:
1 pound bacon, in one piece
12 small white onions, peeled
3 tablespoons bacon drippings
Freshly ground black pepper
1 pound lentils
1 carrot, quartered
1 rib celery
4 hard-cooked eggs, quartered
1 sprig of fresh dill
1 bay leaf
2 sprays parsley
3 cloves garlic, minced
⅓ cup chopped parsley

Boil the bacon for about 15 minutes, rinse, and pat dry. Brown the onions in hot bacon drippings. Add the bacon to the rest of the ingredients, except the parsley, cover with water, and simmer for two hours or until tender. Remove the bacon and slice. Strain the lentils and remove all the extraneous bits, celery, etc. Arrange the lentils and the onions in the center of a platter and surround with bacon slices and hard-cooked-egg quarters and sprinkle chopped parsley over all. Serves 4.

Köttbullar—Swedish meat balls

TIME: 2 HOURS

There is, of course, good chopped meat and poor, but what seems to matter the most is how it is cooked. It is an astonishment and delight to sample the ways meat balls vary in flavor, texture, and ways in which they are cooked from country to country. All seem good. This particular delicately seasoned version, from a friend who grew up in Sweden and now lives in Copenhagen, is especially good. Certainly the first time I tasted them in the more sophisticated cocktail size, I ate them steadily and greedily, managing to be near the plate each time a fresh, hot batch was brought from the kitchen. Good manners and my usual modest capacity were completely forgotten. When her sister makes gravy she puts in a little sherry for taste, about 3 tablespoons. Her sister has been known to use whiskey. She said that she has heard a little beer does no harm.

Menu: KÖTTBULLAR
       BAKED POTATOES
       PRESSED CUCUMBERS
       BROILED GRAPEFRUIT HALVES
       COFFEE

KÖTTBULLAR:

¾ pound good lean beef, ground
¼ pound lean veal, ground
¼ pound pork, medium fat (ground at least 2, preferably
  3, times)
1 large or 2 small egg yolks
1 whole egg
¾ cup milk or cream
1 Holland rusk, crushed fine with rolling pin
Salt and pepper
1 teaspoon sugar
1 medium-sized yellow onion (if desired)

Mix eggs, milk, rusk crumbs, salt and pepper, and sugar and let stand for about ¾ hour in a large bowl. Then beat the meats into mixture with a wooden spoon. This should take about 10 minutes or until mixture is fluffy. With wet hands shape into meat balls size of a small egg or a rather large walnut. Place meat balls on a large platter as they are formed. Brown in butter in a skillet at high heat. When brown all over, turn down heat, cover, and simmer over very low heat, turning now and then and watching to prevent burning, for about 30 minutes. If onion is used, slice thin and put over meat balls as soon as they are browned. Water should not be added, but if gravy is wanted, transfer meat balls from pan, and keep warm, add 1 teaspoon flour and 1 cup liquid (½ water, ½ cream) to drippings and stir. Serves 4.

Mussel casserole, Italian style

TIME: 1¼ HOURS

Louis Morino, who owns and runs the famous sea-food restaurant in downtown New York known, rather inelegantly, as "Sloppy Louie's" is one of the authorities on preparing mussels, and is a man dedicated to converting all non-mussel eaters to this gastronomic bliss. He advises caution in the amount of rosemary unless accustomed to it.

Menu: MUSSEL CASSEROLE
RAW BROCCOLI WITH GARLIC MAYONNAISE
FRENCH OR ITALIAN BREAD
CHEESE AND MELBA TOAST
COFFEE

MUSSEL CASSEROLE:

4 pounds mussels, scrubbed clean
1 medium-sized onion, chopped
1 tablespoon chopped parsley
½ teaspoon fresh rosemary leaves, chopped (double this if you know you like it, halve it for the dried)
⅔ cups olive oil
½ cup dry white wine
Salt and pepper

Let cold water run over the mussels for a half hour, then plunge into lukewarm water for 2 minutes. They will open and close and wash themselves out. Throw away any that are floating on top. Scrub the shells with a stiff brush. Sauté the onion, parsley, and rosemary until golden brown. Put in a casserole with the mussels, shells and all. Bake in a 300° oven for about 10 minutes. Add the wine, salt and pepper and cook for 5 minutes more. Pull off the top shells (the top shell is the half that doesn't have the mussel attached to it). Serve the bottom shells with the mussels in large warm soup plates with the juices poured over them. Have plenty of French bread to mop up the juices and give everyone an extra plate to put the shells into. Serves 4 blissfully.

126

Pebre (Chilean)

TIME: 1 HOUR FOR CHILLING

This is a highly seasoned, sloshy sort of salad, somewhat like a *gazpacho* but less liquid.

Menu: THICK BROILED STEAK
  BAKED POTATOES
  PEBRE
  HOT ROLLS
  LEMON PUDDING
  COFFEE

PEBRE:

  3 *Spanish onions, peeled and chopped fine*
  3 *medium-sized tomatoes, cubed*
  1 *ají, or hot green pepper chopped fine (the canned hot green Mexican peppers may be bought in a store that carries Mexican food)*
  3 *tablespoons olive oil*
  1 *tablespoon vinegar*
  Salt and pepper
  Lettuce leaves

Mix the onion, tomatoes, hot green pepper together. Blend the oil and vinegar, salt and pepper, and pour over the onion and tomato mixture. Chill slightly before serving mounded on lettuce leaves. Serves 4.

Shirred eggs (oeufs sur le plat—French)

TIME: 20 MINUTES

The French like shirred eggs and make them as well and almost as often as they do omelets. Sometimes they are cooked plain, sometimes served with black butter sauce, other times a few tablespoons of cream are put in the bottom of the dish, or chopped spinach, or a slice of bacon and/or a slice of cheese—the variations are without limit. It is necessary to have some small, individual casseroles, just large enough to hold one or two eggs. The French ones, shallow and usually white, are called *cocottes*. The old-fashioned white-ridged custard cup will do if there are some of those around. While the eggs are served for a light meal, either at lunch or supper, the French practically never serve them for breakfast as we do.

Menu: OEUFS SUR LE PLAT
SALADE NIÇOISE (see page 70)
FRENCH BREAD
WINE JELLY
MACAROONS
COFFEE

OEUFS SUR LE PLAT:
1 teaspoon melted butter
2 eggs for each person
Salt
Embellishments—black butter (browned butter with a few drops of vinegar, salt and pepper), a slice of bacon, a slice of cheese for each dish, mashed chicken livers with crumbled, cooked bacon, or chopped, cooked spinach with a drop or two of lemon juice, or just heavy cream.

Melt the butter and pour into the bottom of a cocotte. Add one of the embellishments if desired. Break the eggs and slide into the dish. Put into a 370° oven for 4 minutes or until the whites are set. Salt and garnish with black butter, chicken livers, sausage, or what you will. Salt added before cooking appears unappetizing. Serves 1.

128

Polenta with Parmesan or Romano cheese and fried onions (Italian)

TIME: 1 HOUR

In Northern Italy polenta is served with the same sauces that are used on pasta farther South, but often it is simply dressed as in this version.

Menu: POLENTO WITH PARMESAN OR ROMANO CHEESE AND FRIED
ONIONS

ARTICHOKES WITH ONION AND DILL (see page 49)

FRENCH OR ITALIAN BREAD

STEWED FRESH PEARS WITH THIN CUSTARD SAUCE, PREF-
ERABLY A ZABAGLIONE

COFFEE

POLENTA WITH PARMESAN OR ROMANO
CHEESE AND FRIED ONIONS:

2 cups corn meal

2 teaspoons salt

5 cups boiling water

3 tablespoons grated Parmesan or Romano cheese

4 onions, peeled and sliced thin

3 tablespoons olive oil

½ cup more grated Parmesan or Romano cheese

Stir the corn meal into the salted boiling water in a large pot, adding it by the handful and turning the heat down low after each addition so that it will not splutter over you. Stir until smooth and thick. Add the grated cheese and stir that around. Turn into a buttered mold and let set awhile. Meanwhile sauté the onions in the olive oil until pale yellow and cooked through but still crisp. Unmold the polenta and cut in thick slices by holding a string taut between the two hands. Arrange the slices in a circle on a hot earthenware platter, top with the sautéed onion rings, and sprinkle the rest of the grated cheese on top. Serves 4 to 6.

Paella (Spanish)

TIME: 2½ HOURS

Paella is the Spanish and Latin-American dish of chicken and rice and seafood and whatever suits the mood and is indigenous to the country. This is Nina Ayala's version. She is Chilean, married to a Spaniard, who has lived in Spain, Argentina and Brazil in addition to her own country. She says that this is the dish as cooked in Spain.

Menu: PAELLA
FLAN (A FINE EUROPEAN CUSTARD)
STRONG DARK COFFEE

PAELLA:

2 onions, peeled and chopped
2 cloves garlic, minced
3 tablespoons olive oil
3½-pound chicken, cut up for frying
1 large can tomatoes
Salt
3 tablespoons chopped parsley
1 chorizo (the hot Spanish sausage), cut in pieces
½ teaspoon saffron, soaked in ⅓ cup boiling water
1 teaspoon orégano
⅔ pound cleaned but uncooked shrimp
1 cup uncooked rice
1 cup cooked fresh green peas
1 can hearts of artichokes, drained
1 tin pimientos, drained and cut into pieces

Sauté the onion and garlic in the olive oil in the bottom of a Dutch oven. Add the pieces of chicken and cook until brown. Add the tomatoes, salt, chopped parsley and cook until the chicken is tender. Add the chorizo, saffron, orégano, and shrimp. Simmer a bit and add the rice to the mixture with 2 cups water. Bring to a boil, cover, turn heat down low, and cook 15 to 20 minutes until the rice is tender. Remove the cover, fluff with a fork, and cook a little longer if necessary. The rice should be very dry and flaky. Add lots of salt at this time and the peas and artichokes and pimientos. Serve in an earthenware casserole. Serves 4 to 6.

Potato cakes (roesti—Swiss)

TIME: 1¼ HOURS

In Switzerland, according to Lucy Glarner, married to Fritz, who is half Swiss, one of the favorite regional dishes is a potato cake browned through and through.

Menu: SAUSAGE
ROESTI
SALAD: MIXED GREENS AND SLICED TOMATOES WITH A DRESSING (2 PARTS OLIVE OIL, 1 PART GARLIC VINEGAR, SALT AND PEPPER)
ROQUEFORT CHEESE AND FRENCH BREAD
COFFEE

ROESTI:
¼ pound butter or lard
6 large potatoes, boiled, peeled, and grated coarsely
Salt and pepper

Melt the butter in a large skillet, add the grated potatoes, unseat from the bottom and brown. Keep turning the potatoes around so that each part of the potatoes gets crisp and brown. Serve on a hot plate. Serves 4 to 6 generously.

Persian meat balls—kaufta

TIME: 2 HOURS

In Persia, or rather Iran, light, fluffy, herb-flavored meat balls are cooked and served in a heavy gruel made of *pirda,* which is what they call coarsely cracked wheat and others call *boulgour.*

Menu: KAUFTA
   SWEET AND SOUR GREEN BEANS (COOKED GREEN BEANS MARINATED IN A LITTLE OF THE COOKING WATER, JUICE OF 1 LEMON AND SOME SUGAR AND 1 CUP SOUR CREAM WITH 1 EGG YOLK BEATEN INTO IT)
   CORN MUFFINS
   SLICES OF COLD WATERMELON
   COFFEE

132

KAUFTA:

1½ cups pirda (boulgour), coarse grind
1 medium-sized onion, chopped fine
Butter
2 pounds veal, cut in small pieces and then pounded in
a mortar until it becomes a paste
Salt
½ teaspoon dried mint or 1 teaspoon finely chopped fresh
½ teaspoon tarragon or 1 teaspoon finely chopped fresh
Paprika

Cook the pirda in 4 cups heavily salted water for about 45 minutes, adding more water if necessary. It should be about the consistency of bean soup. Sauté the onion in butter, mix with the veal paste, salt, mint, tarragon, and paprika. Make into meat balls about the size of a tennis ball. Add the meat balls to the pirda and cook about 30 to 40 minutes. Serve in bowls in the sauce. Serves 4 to 6.

Raw potato pancakes (German)

TIME: 1 HOUR

A friend of Hungarian background has lived in Germany and Vienna for a long while. She says that in these countries there is no nonsense about potatoes being just an accompaniment to the main course; they're a dessert, too. This one is often served with either applesauce or lemon juice and sugar for dessert. When served with a main dish, 1 small onion finely chopped is added to the batter, and, of course, the applesauce omitted.

Menu: HOT BORSCHT
      RYE BREAD
      RAW POTATO PANCAKES WITH APPLESAUCE
      COFFEE

RAW POTATO PANCAKES:
      6 medium-sized potatoes, peeled and grated
      3 eggs
      Salt and pepper
      1 to 2 tablespoons fine bread crumbs or matzoh meal
      3 tablespoons oil

Mix the grated potatoes with the eggs, salt and pepper, and bread crumbs or meal into a thin batter. Sauté in oil heated until a few drops of water dance when flicked into the pan. Fry a few at a time. Serves 4.

Lamb and okra stew, Armenian style

TIME: 1½ HOURS

Such disparate peoples as our Southerners and those living around the Mediterranean cook okra lovingly and often. In stews its clear green and gelatinous texture add an unordinary look and taste.

Menu: LAMB AND OKRA STEW
    TOSSED GREEN SALAD WITH FRENCH DRESSING (2 PARTS OLIVE OIL, 1 PART TARRAGON VINEGAR, SALT AND PEPPER)
    HOT CORN BREAD
    PLUM UPSIDE-DOWN CAKE
    COFFEE

LAMB AND OKRA STEW, ARMENIAN STYLE:
    1 pound small, tender okra, or one large can, drained
    Salt and pepper
    2 large onions, sliced
    1 pound lamb, cut up for stew
    2 tablespoons fat
    3 fresh tomatoes, peeled and cut in small pieces
    1 lemon, cut in thin slices, seed removed but not peeled

Wash the okra and put in a bowl. Sprinkle with salt and pepper. Let stand for a while. Brown the onions and the lamb in fat in a Dutch oven or a deep, heavy skillet. Add 3 cups water, cover and simmer for 1 hour. Add the okra, tomatoes, and lemon, cook over low heat until okra is tender but not mushy. The canned okra takes much less time. Serves 4.

Roumanian fried beans (iahnie de fasole)

TIME: 12 HOURS; 24 HOURS IF SOAKED OVERNIGHT

I've always liked cooking beans, partly because they need no shelling or peeling or any other such tedious preparation, but Roumanians can even make cooking beans a production and make it worth the bother. The beans are soaked and the skins pinched off because they are much more delicate this way, according to them. They will even keep the shells in a paper bag to impress the guests with how much loving care went into the dish cooked for them.

Menu: BAKED PORK CHOPS
IAHNIE DE FASOLE
RAW BROCCOLI SERVED WITH AOLI (MAYONNAISE MADE
WITH 2 OR 3 CLOVES GARLIC)
LEMON CHIFFON PUDDING
COFFEE

IAHNIE DE FASOLE:

1 pound marrow beans, soaked
2 large onions, chopped
2 tablespoons olive oil
1 cup bouillon
2 tablespoons finely chopped dill
2 fresh tomatoes, chopped, seeds removed
Salt

Pinch the skins off the beans, which have been soaked 4 hours or overnight. Cover with water, bring to a boil, drain off this water, add some fresh, and cook until tender but not mushy. Sauté the onions in the oil until pale yellow, add the beans and a little of the bean water. Add the bouillon gradually until almost soupy. Add the dill, tomatoes, and a little salt, remembering that the bouillon has some. Simmer until some of the liquid has cooked down. Let cool slightly before serving. This is a good Lenten dish. Serves 4.

Rognons liégeois (lamb kidneys cooked in gin— Belgian)

TIME: 15 MINUTES

Living practically next door to the Dutch, who make the best of all gin, smooth, soft and potent, the Belgians think it natural to cook with it, and even to add for emphasis a few of the juniper berries that flavor the gin. To get in the right spirit or spirits for the dish, drink a glass of the Holland gin, or *genever,* as it is called there, icy-cold and straight. This is not the gin to be diluted or mixed with anything else. Naturally the gin used in cooking will have lost its alcoholic content though keeping its flavor. And, of course, any kind of gin may be used in cooking.

Menu: ROGNONS LIÉGEOIS
       BRAISED ENDIVE (see page 157)
       GRATIN DE POMME DE TERRE À LA DAUPHINOIS (see page
         100)
       FRESH RASPBERRIES AND PINEAPPLE CHUNKS
       COFFEE

ROGNONS LIÉGEOIS:
    8 lamb kidneys
    4 tablespoons unsalted butter
    Salt and pepper
    4 ponies gin
    18 juniper berries slightly crushed

Sauté the kidneys whole over high heat in 2 tablespoons of the butter, heated until sizzling, for about 3 minutes, add the salt and pepper, lower the heat, add 3 ponies of the gin, cover, and simmer about 2 minutes. Add the crushed juniper berries, the rest of the gin, cover, and simmer for 5 minutes more, add the rest of the unsalted butter, stir around until melted. Serve at once. Serves 4.

Risotto Milanese (Italian)

TIME: 1 HOUR

After you have once eaten a *risotto,* cooked lovingly in butter, then in broth, and artfully seasoned, plain boiled rice can taste awfully flat, flavorless, and boring. And as a matter of fact it is.

Menu: BROILED CHICKEN BREAST, BASTED WITH BUTTER AND
TARRAGON
RISOTTO MILANESE
SWEET AND SOUR GREEN BEANS (see menu, page 132)
HOT ROLLS
FRESH STRAWBERRIES, WITH SWEETENED WHIPPED CREAM
WITH CURAÇAO
COFFEE

RISOTTO MILANESE:
1 stick butter (½ cup)
1 medium-sized onion, chopped fine
1 cup rice
2 cups chicken broth
½ cup Marsala wine (nice but not obligatory)
½ teaspoon saffron steeped in ¼ cup hot water
Salt and pepper
⅓ cup grated Parmesan or Romano cheese

Melt the butter in a heavy, deep saucepan and sauté the onion until golden brown. Add the rice and cook over a low flame for about 10 or 15 minutes, stirring constantly. Add the broth and wine and saffron, salt and pepper with water. Bring to a boil, turn the flame down low, cover and cook for 20 to 30 minutes until the rice is tender and the broth absorbed. With this amount of butter and a very low flame the rice cannot be overcooked. It also may be cooked ahead of time if you wish to avoid last minute fussing. Stir the grated cheese into the rice just before serving. Serves 4.

Italian stuffed artichokes

TIME: 3 HOURS

Those who like artichokes don't need any additional lure; but for the lazy ones who are not sure that the bother of eating them is worth while for such small return these are good. There is a feeling that you are getting a whole bite from the tip of each leaf.

Menu: FRIKANDELLER (see page 170)
ITALIAN STUFFED ARTICHOKES
RISOTTO MILANESE (see page 138)
HOT DROP BISCUITS
HALVES OF HONEYDEW MELON FILLED WITH BLUEBERRIES
COFFEE

ITALIAN STUFFED ARTICHOKES:

4 large, fat artichokes
⅓ cup freshly grated Parmesan cheese
⅔ cup bread crumbs, homemade if possible
2 tablespoons chopped fresh parsley
2 small cloves garlic, minced, or 1 plump one
Salt and pepper
3 tablespoons olive oil

Pull off the outside leaves of the artichokes, cut off the stem and thorny part from the tips of the leaves. Turn upside-down and pound to open the leaves. Mix the cheese, bread crumbs, parsley, garlic, salt and pepper together. Sprinkle among the leaves and put artichokes upright in a baking dish with 1 inch salted water. Sprinkle the olive oil over the artichokes, cover tightly, and bake in a 325° oven for about 2 to 2½ hours, depending upon the size of the artichokes. They are done when the bottom leaves pull off easily. Serves 4.

Kedgeree (mostly Anglo-Indian)

TIME: 30 MINUTES

Kedgeree always begins with rice and usually is a mishmash of that and boiled fish and heavy cream embellished with sliced hard-cooked eggs, though there are some versions that have lentils instead of the fish. It's an easily improvised dish from ingredients on hand in most larders.

Menu: KEDGEREE
SALAD: CHICORY WITH DICED CUCUMBER AND THIN-SLICED SWEET RED ONIONS WITH A SHARP FRENCH DRESSING (1 PART OLIVE OIL, 1 PART GARLIC VINEGAR, SALT AND PEPPER)
CORN STICKS
COLD, RIPE PLUMS AND CREAM CHEESE
TEA

KEDGEREE:

> 1/4 pound finnan haddie or other salt fish
> 3/4 pound fresh codfish or halibut
> 1 cup uncooked rice
> 1 1/2 teaspoons salt
> 1/4 cup heavy cream or sweet butter
> Salt and pepper
> 1/4 cup finely chopped chives or parsley
> 4 hard-cooked eggs, sliced thin

Simmer the fish together over a low flame until white and opaque. Drain, pick out any bones, and flake. While the fish is simmering, put the rice in a pot with 2 cups water and the salt, bring to a boil, cover tightly, and turn heat down very low. Cook for 14 minutes. Remove lid and fluff the rice with a fork. Add the fish flakes (for unscheduled meals any canned fish may be used). Add the cream or butter, pepper and additional salt if necessary, chopped chives or parsley and mix. Turn into a warm bowl and arrange the slices of hard-cooked egg decoratively on top. Serves 4.

Italian fried green beans

TIME: 45 MINUTES

Jean Lapolla, who has the European feeling that something should be done about vegetables besides just cooking them in water, serves green beans this way, crisp and different and delicious.

Menu: ITALIAN SPAGHETTI WITH MEAT BALLS (see page 60)
ITALIAN FRIED GREEN BEANS
FRENCH OR ITALIAN BREAD
CHEESE
COFFEE

ITALIAN FRIED GREEN BEANS

2 pounds green beans, broken into 2- or 3-inch pieces, cooked the usual way until tender
1 egg, slightly beaten
Flour
Olive oil
Salt and pepper

Dip the green beans a few at a time, first in the beaten egg, and then in the flour. Put olive oil in the skillet about 1 inch or 1½ inches deep, or use your electric deep fryer if you have one. Cook the beans until crisp, drain on paper towels, salt and pepper, and serve very hot. Serves 4.

Pasta e ceci (Italian)

TIME: 12 HOURS FOR DRIED BEANS, 1 HOUR FOR CANNED

This is a variation on the much-loved Italian *pasta e fagioli,* often mispronounced, *"Pasta fazooli."* It is a variable one-dish meal from Southern Italy.

Menu: PASTA E CECI

      MIXED GREEN SALAD WITH FRENCH DRESSING (2 PARTS OLIVE OIL, 1 PART TARRAGON VINEGAR, SALT AND PEPPER)

      ITALIAN OR FRENCH BREAD

      BRANDIED BLACK BING CHERRIES

      COFFEE

PASTA E CECI:

- *1 large onion, chopped fine*
- *2 cloves garlic, minced*
- *½ cup olive oil*
- *2 cups ceci (garbanzos, or chick-peas, whatever you wish to call them), soaked overnight*
- *1 yellow or zucchini squash, cooked and diced*
- *2 cups beef bouillon*
- *1 tomato, chopped and seeded*
- *1 hot green pepper, chopped and seeds removed*
- *1 pound pasta in any of the small shapes, ditalini, tiny shells, bows, or even the larger wagon wheels, etc.*

Cook the onion and the garlic in the oil and transfer to a large pot with the ceci. Cover with water and simmer until the ceci are tender. They will be done when a couple of the slightly cooled ones feel tender when pinched with the fingers. Boil the pasta in salted water 6 or 7 minutes, drain, and add to the beans along with the bouillon, green pepper, squash, and tomato. Cook at a medium boil, which means not too violently or not too lethargically, for about 10 minutes more. Serve poured over a crust of Italian bread or rusk in deep bowls. Serves 4 to 6 amply.

Stuffed cabbage (kåldormar—Swedish)

TIME: 2 HOURS

From the Balkan to the Scandinavian countries leaves of cabbage are stuffed with rice mixed with this and that and cooked in a sauce. The mixture, the flavoring, and the accompanying sauce vary from country to country. This is the Swedish version with mother and daughter styles, or the old and the new. The mother does not hold with this modern nonsense of adding cream to the drippings, though her daughter does, and you can either take it or leave it. Neither the straight drippings nor the cream gravy should have any flour thickening.

Menu: KÅLDORMAR
      CURRANT JELLY
      STRING BEANS
      PUMPERNICKEL
      RED PUDDING (RASPBERRY AND/OR CURRANT JUICE SWEET-
         ENED AND THICKENED SLIGHTLY WITH THE TRADITIONAL
         ARROWROOT OR THE MORE CONVENIENT CORNSTARCH.
         CHILL AND SERVE WITH HEAVY CREAM.)
      COFFEE

KÅLDORMAR:
      1 head white cabbage (not too firm, as the leaves have to come off easily)
      ¾ pound beef, ½ pound veal, ground together 2 or preferably 3 times
      1 egg
      1 cup rice (cooked in milk about ¾ hour, about ⅓ cup raw rice to 1½ cups milk)
      1 teaspoon sugar
      Salt and pepper to taste
      3 tablespoons butter or margarine
      6–8 whole allspice (if desired, not everyone likes the taste)
      ½ cup light cream (nice but not essential)

Soak cabbage head in cold water for 1 hour. Cut off end. Gently detach leaves, making sure not to break them. Boil for 10 to 12 minutes or until tender, but not too soft. Remove from water, drain in colander. Mix meat, egg, cooked rice, sugar, salt and pepper thoroughly. Place a heaping tablespoon of mixture on each cabbage leaf (amount depends somewhat on size of leaf). Roll up, tie with string, or secure with toothpick. Remove string before serving. Brown stuffed rolls in butter or margarine until very brown in frying pan. Remove, place with drippings in Dutch oven. Add allspice. Simmer with lid on (very slow fire) watching and turning constantly for about ½ hour. If gravy is desired, remove cabbage rolls (keep warm), add light cream (about ½ cup) to drippings (no flour), and stir. This recipe will result in about 12 good-sized kåldormar, which will serve 4 generously and 6 adequately.

Cold borscht with improvements (Russian)

TIME: 1 HOUR, MOSTLY FOR CHILLING

Borscht is the good red soup, sometimes thick, sometimes thin, sometimes hot, and sometimes cold. It is always good, whether the hot and complicated kind made with a strong beef stock or the simple cold one with "improvements," the name for the classic garnishes. Cold borscht, with its clear, lovely color, takes little preparation and may be made in quantities and kept in the refrigerator for ready use. With the embellishments and some good French bread or rich, dark pumpernickel it is enough for a light meal on a hot, hot day. I think diced cucumber and chopped spring onions are best in this, topped with a tablespoon of sour cream, but the traditional improvements include slices of hard-cooked eggs and a hot boiled potato in each bowl.

Menu: COLD BORSCHT
SWISS ONION PIE (see page 193)
FRESH PEACH SHORTCAKE
COFFEE

COLD BORSCHT:

6 medium-sized beets, peeled and diced
Juice of ½ lemon
½ large cucumber, peeled and diced
4 to 6 spring onions, cut in pieces
Sour cream
Sliced hard-cooked eggs
4 hot boiled potatoes, peeled

Cook the beets in 5 cups water until tender or a pressure cooker for 3 minutes. Add the lemon juice and the color will immediately go back into the beets, which had become pale and depressing-looking. If you are in a hurry, it is possible to cheat a little and use a can of diced cooked beets, diluting the juice with water or chicken broth and adding lemon juice. Chill. When ready to serve, pour into cold pretty soup bowls, add the chopped cucumber and spring onion and any of the other improvements you wish. Top with a dollop of sour cream. When the hot potatoes are used, one is placed in the soup bowl and the cold soup poured over it. Serves 4.

German egg cake (eierkuchen)

TIME: 1¼ HOURS

This German version of a baked omelet is more like a cake than ones called this in other countries. It is served with cranberry sauce or currant or some other tart jelly for lunch or a light supper.

Menu: EIERKUCHEN
SWEET AND SOUR GREEN BEANS (see menu, page 132)
HOT POPPY-SEED ROLLS
HOT RASPBERRIES (WARM IN OVEN IN THEIR OWN JUICE)
THIN OATMEAL COOKIES
COFFEE

EIERKUCHEN:
1½ cups sifted flour
½ teaspoon baking powder
½ teaspoon salt
3 eggs, beaten
1 cup milk

Add the flour, baking powder, and salt little by little to the eggs and milk beaten together. Pour into a shallow, buttered tin or casserole. Bake for 1 hour in a slow 325° oven. When done, cut in squares and serve with cranberry sauce or currant jelly.

Cocido, Argentine version

TIME: 3 HOURS COOKING, OVERNIGHT SOAKING

In Argentina squash and corn are added to the traditional Spanish ingredients and very fine noodles are served in the soup, which is served separately, as is the Spanish *cocido* or the French *pot-au-feu*. The broth is served first, with the meat and vegetables as the main course.

Menu: COCIDO
      HOT CORN BREAD
      FRESH GRAPES
      CHEESE
      COFFEE

COCIDO:
> 1 pound chick peas, soaked overnight
> 1 blood sausage, obtainable in groceries catering to a foreign clientele
> 1 chorizo
> 1 pound stew beef, in one piece
> ¼ pound bacon, in one piece
> 3 potatoes, peeled and quartered
> ½ head cabbage, cut in wedges
> 1 yellow squash or zucchini, cut into thick slices but not peeled
> Fresh corn cut from 3 ears
> Salt and pepper
> Very fine noodles

Simmer the chick-peas with the blood sausage, chorizo, beef, and bacon in water more than to cover. Bring to a boil, skim. Bring to another boil, skim. Repeat until there is nothing more to skim. Simmer about 2 hours or until the meat and the chick peas are tender. Add the potatoes, cabbage, cook for 20 to 30 minutes until almost tender, add the zucchini and corn, salt and pepper and cook for about 5 to 10 minutes more. Boil the noodles until tender. Serve the broth first, and then the vegetables. Serves 6 to 8.

Fried eggs served Persian-fashion

TIME: 45 MINUTES

For the gastronomically open-minded (and you must be, or why are you reading this book?) this recipe is a pleasant change from the good but usual fried eggs and bacon or ham. It is fine for lunch, a very late supper, or Sunday breakfast.

Menu: FRIED EGGS SERVED PERSIAN-FASHION
      HOT FRENCH BREAD, THE BROWN-AND-SERVE KIND
      COFFEE GELATIN WITH THIN CHOCOLATE WAFERS
      COFFEE
      (FOR SUNDAY BREAKFAST SERVE STRAWBERRIES AND PINE-
         APPLE CHUNKS AS A FIRST COURSE AND OMIT THE
         GELATIN.)

FRIED EGGS SERVED PERSIAN-FASHION:
*1 pound hot, fresh-cooked asparagus or string beans, or
   1 box frozen
8 eggs, fried in butter
½ stick butter, or ⅛ pound
1 clove garlic, minced
1 cup yoghurt
Salt and paprika*

Arrange the asparagus or string beans on a platter or individual plates, with the eggs on top, in an arrangement pleasing to the eye. Cook the garlic slowly in the butter, add the yoghurt, salt and paprika. Mix and pour over the eggs and green vegetable. Serve immediately to 4.

Lamb and beans (gigot aux flageolets—French)

TIME: 3 TO 4 HOURS

According to Escoffier, a prolonged soaking of dried vegetables may give rise to incipient germination and this, by impairing the principles of the vegetables, depreciates the value of the food and may even cause harm to the diner. He does say that if the vegetables are old or inferior in quality (but *not* how to determine this by looking at them) it is permissible to soak them in water with soda long enough to swell them slightly (about 1½ hours). You may follow Escoffier if you wish, or just normal procedure in which beans are soaked without the soda.

Menu: GIGOT AUX FLAGEOLETS
WATER CRESS SALAD WITH ANY GOOD FRENCH DRESSING (2 PARTS OLIVE OIL, 1 PART VINEGAR, SALT AND PEPPER)
FRENCH BREAD
FRESH PEACHES WITH BRANDIED BLACK BING CHERRIES
COFFEE

GIGOT AUX FLAGEOLETS:
1 leg of lamb (5 to 7 pounds; mutton is traditional in Brittany, but not so often available here, at least under that name
2 cloves garlic, minced
3 sprigs fresh rosemary or ½ teaspoon dried
1 pound flageolets or white beans
½ cup white wine
Salt and pepper

Roast the leg of lamb, lightly dusted with flour, or an aromatic, if sparse, bed of garlic. Sprinkle the rosemary on top. Put in a 300° oven, allowing 30 to 35 minutes per pound for lamb and 40 to 45 minutes for mutton. Simmer the beans, covered with water, with an onion, a bay leaf, salt and pepper. Unsoaked, they take about the same time as the lamb. When the meat is done, transfer it to a hot platter and add the white wine to the juices in the pan. Stir in some salt and pepper. Simmer for a bit until well blended. Surround the lamb with the cooked flageolets and pour the lamb gravy and wine over the beans. Serves 6 to 8.

Anchovy and potato pudding (Swedish)

TIME: 1¼ HOURS

This is a simple but unusual dish pleasing to anyone who has a fondness for anchovies, and the ingredients may be kept on hand.

Menu: BROILED SALMON STEAKS
    SWEDISH ANCHOVY AND POTATO PUDDING
    SALAD: MIXED GREENS, SLICED SWEET RED ONIONS, SLICED
        RADISHES WITH FRENCH DRESSING (2 PARTS OLIVE OIL,
        1 PART GARLIC VINEGAR, SALT AND PEPPER)

ANCHOVY AND POTATO PUDDING:
    4 large potatoes, peeled and sliced
    ½ can anchovy fillets, cut in half
    2 eggs
    2 cups milk

In a shallow buttered casserole arrange a layer of raw potato slices and dot sparingly with pieces of anchovy. Add another layer of potatoes, some more anchovies, and repeat until all the ingredients are used. Beat the eggs slightly and add the milk. Pour over the potatoes and bake in a 350° oven until the potatoes are tender. No salt is needed because of the anchovies. Serves 4.

Polish potato soup

TIME: 2 HOURS

Polish potato soup varies from other potato soups mostly in its seasonings, so different and so delectable.

Menu: POLISH POTATO SOUP
    HOT POPPY-SEED ROLLS (BROWN AND SERVE)
    SALMON SALAD (FLAKED SALMON, DICED CUCUMBER,
       CHOPPED ONION, SLICED RADISH, AND PINEAPPLE CHUNKS
       WITH FRENCH DRESSING [2 PARTS OLIVE OIL, 1 PART
       VINEGAR, SALT AND PEPPER])
    HONEYDEW MELON BALLS IN CHILLED WHITE WINE
    COFFEE

POLISH POTATO SOUP:
    6 medium-sized potatoes, diced
    2 large or 4 medium-sized onions, diced
    6 bay leaves
    1 tablespoon whole cloves
    1 quart milk, warmed
    Salt and pepper
    1 teaspoon tarragon vinegar

152

Simmer the potatoes, onions, bay leaves, and cloves happily together in barely enough water to cover until both the potatoes and onions are tender and mushy. Fish out the cloves and bay leaves, add the warm milk, salt and pepper. Add the tarragon vinegar, stirring very carefully so it doesn't curdle. Heat, but do not let it boil. Serve immediately. Serves 4.

Asparagus, Italian-fashion

TIME: 45 MINUTES

The Italians, who never get bored cooking foods the same way, sometimes cook asparagus this way. While asparagus needs no adornment more than melted butter or Hollandaise sauce, this does taste very good.

Menu: PIZZA (see page 94)
     ASPARAGUS, ITALIAN-FASHION
     FRENCH OR ITALIAN BREAD
     STEWED PEARS WITH LEMON SAUCE
     COFFEE

ASPARAGUS, ITALIAN-FASHION:
    1 bunch fresh asparagus
    2 tablespoons olive oil
    1 clove garlic, cut in halves
    Salt and pepper
    2 whole eggs

Wash the asparagus and break off the woody white part. It will break naturally where the tender part begins. Steam the bunch of asparagus in ¾ cup boiling water in either a skillet so that it can lie down, or the bottom half of a double boiler so that it can stand up. When almost tender, after about 10 or 12 minutes, pour out half the water, add the olive oil, garlic, salt and pepper, and the two raw eggs, stir slightly with a fork while finishing cooking. Serve in this mixture, removing the garlic halves first. Serves 4.

Italian sardine pie

TIME: 45 MINUTES

From time to time in other places anything and everything is put in a pie, and sometimes there isn't even a crust.

Menu: ITALIAN SARDINE PIE
FRENCH OR ITALIAN BREAD
SALAD: COOKED BROCCOLI WITH STRIPS OF PIMIENTO,
FRENCH DRESSING (3 PARTS OLIVE OIL, 1 PART VINEGAR,
SALT AND PEPPER)
ORANGE SHERBET
COFFEE

ITALIAN SARDINE PIE: *SPRAT PIE*

19 Sprats *16 sardines (around 4 inches long), drained and the oil
saved (traditionally made from fresh sardines, but not
easily obtainable here)*
1 cup stale, coarse bread crumbs
Salt and pepper
1/3 cup finely chopped parsley
2 cloves garlic, chopped fine
Juice of 1 lemon

Put a layer of sardines, neatly arranged, in a shallow casserole (the casserole first oiled with the sardine oil). Toss together the bread crumbs, seasoning, parsley, and garlic. Sprinkle over the sardines and add a sprinkling of the sardine oil. Add another layer of sardines and top with the bread-crumb mixture and sardine oil. The casserole should be of a size to permit 8 sardines to lie flat in one layer. Bake in a 350° oven 20 to 30 minutes. Remove from the oven. Dribble the lemon juice over all and serve to 4.

Jack Spratt Salad.
Sliced Tomatoes on lettuce
Place on this severd sardine

154

Z. S.

Erwtensoep met worst en kluif (Dutch pea soup)

TIME: 12 HOURS, MORE IF ALLOWED TO SOAK OVERNIGHT

All the cold and cool months of the year the Dutch eat happily and almost daily their good, thick split-pea soup. Because traditionally this soup should be so thick that a spoon will stand straight up in it, the accompanying menu is made light to suit our less robust ways of eating. The Dutch prefer to use Gelderland sausage made from smoked pork, available sometimes in stores with German or Dutch trade, though one version of this soup lists beef sausage. Other times mettwurst is used as one of the ingredients.

Menu: ERWTENSOEP MET WORST EN KLUIF
   ROUMANIAN GREEN PEPPER SALAD (see page 21)
   FRENCH BREAD, CUT IN HUNKS, TOASTED AND BUTTERED
   FRESH CONCORD GRAPE PIE
   COFFEE

ERWTENSOEP MET WORST EN KLUIF:
  2 cups split green peas
  Salt
  2 pig's feet
  3 leeks, chopped
  ½ pound bacon, in one piece
  ½ pound sausage (see above)

Soak the peas overnight in cold water, drain, cover with fresh cold water, and bring to a boil, add the salt, pig's feet, leeks, and celery. Simmer for 3 or 4 hours, or cook 15 minutes at 15 pounds pressure. The peas should not be puréed, but should have an individual look. About ½ hour before serving add the sausage. To serve, remove and slice the cooked sausage, cut the meat from pig's feet, and slice the bacon. Return meats to the soup. Serves 4 to 6.

Callos Mondrago (Spanish)

TIME: 9 HOURS

This lacks the pallid appearance, the blandness, and slippery texture of most tripe dishes that perhaps is responsible for their lack of appeal to many people. Cooked this way, with hot, fiery chorizos, it has savor and a textural interest that will please and confuse. Traditionally this is served in Spain with French-fried potatoes, fruit and cheese and hard rolls—much the same shape and texture as the Pepperidge Farm Brown & Serve club rolls.

Menu: CALLOS MONDRAGO
      FRENCH-FRIED POTATOES
      FRUIT AND CHEESE
      STRONG, DARK COFFEE

CALLOS MONDRAGO
    2 pounds tripe, cut into 1½-inch pieces
    1 onion, sliced
    1 clove garlic, minced
    1 bay leaf
    8 to 10 peppercorns
    1 tablespoon salt
    ⅓ cup olive oil
    2 large onions, sliced
    1 clove garlic, minced
    ¼ pound ham, cut in small pieces
    1 chorizos, about 4 inches long, cut in pieces
    1 teaspoon orégano
    1 large can tomatoes
    3 or 4 pimientos, cut in large pieces

Simmer the tripe, 1 onion, 1 clove garlic and bay leaf, peppercorn and salt in about 1 quart water for 2 or 3 hours until tender. Sauté in olive oil in a casserole the onions, the other garlic, ham, chorizos, and orégano. Add the tomatoes and pimientos. Drain the tripe and add to the sauce. Cook for 4 to 5 hours more. Remove the bay leaf before serving. This cannot be overcooked and if it has simmered gently in and out of the sauce for 9 hours it is best. Serves 4 to 6.

Braised Belgian endive

TIME: 45 MINUTES

In Belgium, when they like a dish, they eat it often. One they eat practically all the time, practically everywhere, is endive, called *witloof* there. They prefer to cook it gently, subtly lessening the slightly bitter tang of this beautiful, smooth, pale, satiny, and elegantly tapered green.

Menu: ERWTENSOEP MET WORST EN KLUIF (see page 155)
BRAISED BELGIAN ENDIVE (SERVE AS A SEPARATE COURSE)
LEMON SHERBET WITH CRISP MOLASSES COOKIES
COFFEE

BRAISED BELGIAN ENDIVE:
1 tablespoon Belgian endive
2 tablespoons lemon juice
3 tablespoons butter
Salt

Rinse the heads of endive in cold water, shake dry, and arrange side by side in a large skillet. Add the lemon juice, 2 tablespoons of the butter, ⅓ cup cold water, and salt. Cover and simmer until tender, about 30 to 40 minutes, adding more water if necessary. Transfer to a hot, shallow casserole, cook the liquid in the pan until reduced to about half, add 1 tablespoon more butter, and pour over the endive. Serves 4 to 6.

Bauernschmaus (sauerkraut with dumplings and meat—German)

TIME: 1 HOUR

This lusty German dish honoring sauerkraut charms even the most lukewarm admirers of this food. Traditionally sliced roast pork, a sausage called *Selchkarnee,* and *Bratwurst* are cooked with this, but, lacking a good German delicatessen, probably just pork and Bratwurst might do. The dumplings, called *Knödeln,* that go with this are especially good.

Menu: BAUERNSCHMAUS
RYE BREAD, IF THE DUMPLINGS AREN'T SUFFICIENT
FRUIT COMPOTE OF STEWED PEARS AND RASPBERRIES
COFFEE

DUMPLINGS:
>1 onion, finely chopped
>1 tablespoon fat
>2 tablespoons finely chopped parsley
>1½ tablespoons flour
>1 teaspoon salt
>1 cup milk
>1 egg, beaten
>4 to 6 slices stale bread, cut in cubes

Gravy:
>3 tablespoons fat from the sausage
>3 tablespoons flour
>1½ cups beef stock or bouillon

BAUERNSCHMAUS:
>2 pounds sauerkraut, preferably the kind that comes in a barrel
>Sliced roast pork
>Selchkarnee
>Bratwurst, crisply fried
>Knödeln (dumplings)
>Flour

For the dumplings sauté the onion in the fat, add the parsley, flour, salt, blend, and add the milk and egg beaten together and the dry bread cubes. Mix together and drop in by the spoonful into boiling salted water for 6 to 8 minutes. Drain. For the sauce sauté the sausage, remove from the skillet, and pour off all the fat except about 3 tablespoons. Add the flour, blend well, and add the stock, slowly stirring until smooth. Drain the sauerkraut and add enough flour to its juice to make a sauce the consistency of cream. Put the sauerkraut in a heavy casserole, add the sliced roast pork, sausage, Selchkarnee, Bratwurst, and dumplings and pour the thickened sauerkraut juice and gravy over all. Serves 4.

Roumanian cucumber salad

TIME: 1 HOUR, INCLUDING CHILLING TIME

It's just the preparation and the seasoning that makes this cucumber salad a little different from, and a little better than, many others.

Menu: BROILED FRESH SALMON STEAKS
BROCCOLI WITH HOLLANDAISE
TINY NEW POTATOES COOKED AND SERVED IN THEIR SKINS
HOT BISCUITS
ROUMANIAN CUCUMBER SALAD
LEMON TARTS
COFFEE

ROUMANIAN CUCUMBER SALAD:
1 large cucumber
French dressing (2 parts olive oil, 1 part wine vinegar, salt and pepper)
2 tablespoons finely chopped fresh dill

Slice the cucumber paper-thin on large-grooved grater, so that it is almost shredded. Drain and pat dry with a towel. Marinate in the French dressing, sprinkle lavishly with the fresh dill, and chill. Serves 2 to 3.

Potato and cheese casserole (Belgian)

TIME: 1 HOUR

This is a pleasing version of a much-loved European combination, but much simpler to prepare than the French one.

Menu: BAKED PORK CHOPS
POTATO AND CHEESE CASSEROLE
BELGIAN TOMATO SALAD (see page 98)
BLUEBERRY TART
COFFEE

POTATO AND CHEESE CASSEROLE:

2 tablespoons butter
5 large potatoes, peeled and sliced thin
1 cup grated cheese, Swiss is traditional but good Cheddar will do as well
2 eggs, beaten with 2 cups milk
Salt and pepper

160

Melt the butter in the bottom of a casserole. Put a layer of the potatoes, sprinkle generously with the cheese, salt and pepper. Repeat until all these ingredients are used. Pour over the eggs beaten with the milk. Let sit on the top of the stove for about 5 minutes then place in a 350° oven and bake 30 minutes or until the potatoes are tender and the dish a little custardy looking. Serves 4.

Syrian lentil soup

TIME: 2½ HOURS

This is a sturdy but fresh-tasting soup much like the Italian dish of *fave* and spinach.

Menu: SYRIAN LENTIL SOUP
        SMALL CHERRY TOMATOES
        FRENCH OR ITALIAN BREAD
        FRESH PLUM TART
        COFFEE

SYRIAN LENTIL SOUP:

> 2 cups lentils
> 2 medium-sized onions, sliced thin
> 3 tablespoons olive oil
> ½ pound fresh spinach washed thoroughly, patted dry, and
>   chopped coarsely, or ½ package frozen
> Salt
> Lemon juice
> Sour cream, if desired

Cover the lentils with water and cook until tender, about 1½ hours. Sauté the onions in the olive oil, add to the lentils, and cook for about ½ hour more. Add the spinach and salt and cook 15 to 20 minutes longer. Just before serving stir in the lemon juice. Top each serving with a spoonful of sour cream if desired. Serves 4 to 6.

Fritto misto alla Romana (Italian)

TIME: 1 HOUR

One of the most delicate, delectable, and unfussy of all ways of presenting leftovers. Bits of this and that, sort of odds and ends of foods are deep-fried and served together crisp, golden, and anonymous-looking.

Menu: FRITTO MISTO ALLA ROMANA
       TOSSED GREEN SALAD
       SOUR CHERRY TART
       COFFEE

FRITTO MISTO ALLA ROMANA:

Take any pleasing combination of foods such as this:
Calf's liver, cut in strips and lightly floured
Lamb kidney, cut in pieces, dipped in beaten egg, and then in bread crumbs
Cooked artichoke hearts, dusted with flour, dipped in egg, and then flour again
Cooked string beans, with the egg-flour routine
Sliced green tomatoes, dusted with flour, dipped in egg, and then in bread crumbs
Cooked cauliflower, in the same flour-egg-bread-crumb routine
Thin strips of zucchini, floured, egged and bread-crumbed
Fat for deep-frying (peanut oil has a good, low smoking point, but olive oil is traditional)

Fry in deep fat, following the temperatures for cooked and un-cooked foods. Drain and serve.

Italian oxtail soup

TIME: 4 TO 5 HOURS

Sensible people everywhere who like to eat well and who take the trouble to do so cook their regional versions of oxtail soup. This is an Italian one.

Menu: ITALIAN OXTAIL SOUP
   FRENCH OR ITALIAN BREAD
   SMALL BOILED POTATOES WITH THIN SLICES OF RAW ZUC-
      CHINI MARINATED IN FRENCH DRESSING (2 PARTS OLIVE
      OIL, 1 PART VINEGAR, SALT AND PEPPER)
   FRESH STRAWBERRIES SOAKED IN RED WINE, PARTIALLY
      DRAINED, AND SERVED WITH SOUR CREAM
   COFFEE

ITALIAN OXTAIL SOUP:
   2 tablespoons bacon fat
   2 large oxtails, cut at the joints
   2 slices bacon, diced
   2 cloves garlic, minced
   2 onions, chopped
   4 ribs celery, cut in pieces
   ⅓ cup finely chopped parsley
   2 green peppers, tops and seeds removed, and cut in pieces
   2 cups red wine
   Stock, if necessary
   ½ can Italian tomato paste
   Salt and pepper

Brown the oxtails in the bacon fat. Add the diced bacon, garlic, onions, celery, parsley, and green pepper. Cook until partly tender and slightly browned. Add the red wine, tomato paste, and 1 cup water. Simmer for about 4 hours, skimming off what comes to the top, adding more liquid if necessary, either wine, stock, or water, to maintain a slightly sloshy consistency. Just before serving add salt and pepper. Serves 4 to 6.

Pancakes layered with mushroom filling (palacsinta —Hungarian)

TIME: 1½ HOURS

In Hungary, as in most European countries, there is no nonsense about pancakes being a breakfast food. They are a main dish, a dessert, or any part of a meal you want them to be. Practically any meat or sea food or sweet sauce or cheese concoction may be put between the pancakes or rolled up in them, and so on.

Menu: PALACSINTA
ROUMANIAN CUCUMBER SALAD (see page 159)
FRENCH BREAD
LEMON SOUFFLÉ
COFFEE

PALACSINTA:
Batter:
2 cups sifted flour
1 teaspoon salt
3 eggs, separated
3 cups milk
3 tablespoons melted sweet butter

Filling:
2 tablespoons butter
½ pound fresh mushrooms, sliced thin through the caps
Salt and pepper
½ cup sour cream
1 egg slightly beaten
Butter for pancakes

Mix the flour, salt, and egg yolks together. Beat and add the milk slowly. Stir in the melted butter. Put a lump of butter on an 8-inch skillet and heat until a few drops of water flicked into it dance. Pour 3 or 4 tablespoons of the batter into the hot skillet and cook until the bubbles on top burst, and then turn and cook on the other side until brown. Remove and keep in a warm place and make another and another and so on. These pancakes must be made one at a time and the stack kept warm until ready for the filling. Add more butter, a little at a time, if necessary. For the filling sauté the mushrooms in the butter until pale yellow and tender. Add the salt and pepper and the sour cream, which has been mixed with the slightly beaten egg. Stir all together and put 1 tablespoon on each pancake, stacking them as you go. Put in the oven for about 20 minutes to allow the filling to melt and merge. Serve hot and cut in wedges. Serves 4 to 6 generously.

Eggplant salad (Roumanian)

TIME: 1½ HOURS

Ignorance seems to deprive one of much bliss, certainly as far as eating eggplants goes in this country. We bread and fry the slices and that is usually that. All around the Mediterranean it is a much-loved vegetable. This salad, authentically made but well chilled American-fashion, gives a subtle and unexpected touch to an otherwise American meal.

Menu: BROILED CHICKEN BREASTS
      RISI PISI (RICE COOKED IN CHICKEN BROTH WITH FRESH
         GREEN PEAS AND A LUMP OF BUTTER)
      EGGPLANT SALAD
      PISTACHIO ICE CREAM WITH BITTER-CHOCOLATE SAUCE
      COFFEE

EGGPLANT SALAD:
    1 large eggplant
    Olive oil
    Lemon juice
    Salt
    ⅓ cup finely chopped raw onion

Bake eggplant until soft as a pillow. Remove the skin and drain the bitter liquid, pressing a bit to make sure that it's all out. Mash well, add a few drops of oil and a few drops of lemon juice. Whip until fluffy, adding more oil and more lemon juice from time to time. Add salt, put in a bowl, sprinkle with finely chopped raw onion, and chill well. Serves 4.

Polenta with fresh country pork (Italian)

TIME: 2½ HOURS

In Northern Italy polenta, the Italian version of corn meal mush, is sauced much the same as pasta farther south. This particular one is served only in the winter because no sensible Italian butchers a pig in warm weather.

Menu: POLENTA
CAESAR SALAD
COFFEE CUSTARD
COFFEE

POLENTA:

1½ pounds fresh country pork, cut in pieces
Cracklings from the pork
⅓ to ½ pound fresh mushrooms, sliced
Salt
½ box yellow corn meal

Sauté the stew-sized pieces of pork very slowly, and cook at least 45 minutes to 1 hour. Add the cracklings, the crisp pieces that appear when pork fat has been heated. About 10 minutes before serving add the sliced mushrooms and salt if necessary. Using the proportions on the box for corn meal mush, slowly stir the corn meal into rapidly boiling salted water, stirring all the while and turning down the heat before each addition or it's liable to go "plop" and burn you. It should get stiffer and stiffer as you stir. When it is too stiff to stir any more, pour into some greased molds that might be loaf pans. Let cool until hardened. To serve, remove from buttered molds, place on a platter and slice with a piece of string held taut with both hands. Place the slices of polenta on a platter, cover with sauce, and heat briefly before serving. Serves 4.

Egg cake (aeggekage—Danish)

TIME: 45 MINUTES

Every country has its own good way of making a full meal from eggs. This is the Danish way, and, like most dishes of this type, can be varied according to the ingredients on hand.

Menu: AEGGEKAGE

SALAD: PRESSED CUCUMBERS (RIDGE THE RIND BY PULLING THE PRONGS OF A FORK LENGTHWISE ALL AROUND, SLICE THIN, AND CHILL IN DILUTED TARRAGON VINEGAR WITH SALT AND PEPPER—THE SCANDINAVIANS PRESS THE CUCUMBERS BY PUTTING A PLATE WEIGHTED WITH SOMETHING HEAVY ON THEM FOR 30 OR 40 MINUTES, BUT IT DOESN'T SEEM PARTICULARLY NECESSARY)

FRENCH BREAD

RASPBERRY TART

COFFEE

AEGGEKAGE:

8 to 10 slices lean bacon
6 large eggs
2 teaspoons flour
½ cup milk
Salt and pepper
2 large tomatoes, diced
⅓ cup chopped chives

Dice bacon and sauté in about an 8-inch frying pan. Drain off fat except for about a ¼-inch film and the pieces of bacon in the pan. Separate eggs. Beat whites until stiff. Mix flour, milk, salt and pepper into the yolks. Fold in whites. Pour over bacon. Cook over low flame about ½ hour or until eggs are cooked. Midway strew on top of egg cake cubed tomatoes and chopped chives, which look pretty and taste fine. Serve from the pan with buttered French bread. This will serve 4, but for hungry people allow ½ an aeggekage for each. To vary aeggekage, use chopped cooked ham and diced fresh mushrooms, sautéed in butter, or, omitting bacon and/or ham, pour egg mixture into well-buttered pan. Along with tomatoes and chives top with strips of crisp fried bacon, and mushrooms too, if desired. Sometimes use chopped green peppers instead of chives.

Danish meat balls (Frikadeller)

TIME: 1 HOUR

Now in Denmark the meat balls are the lightest, fluffiest, and tenderest of all. To make them, one needs patience, a strong right arm (or left if left-handed), or else an electric mixer.

Menu: FRIKADELLER
BOILED POTATOES WITH BROWNED BUTTER
PRESSED CUCUMBERS (see menu, page 168)
PUMPERNICKEL
RED PUDDING (THE DANISH RÔDGROD MED FLÔDE, THE
GERMAN ROTHE GRUETZE, THE RUSSIAN KISSEL—PUDDING WITH CREAM—CURRANT AND RASPBERRY JUICE
SWEETENED AND SLIGHTLY THICKENED WITH CORNSTARCH)
COFFEE

FRIKADELLER:

1 pound lean pork
½ pound veal
½ cup flour
1 cup milk
Salt and pepper
2 tablespoons butter

The most important part of this recipe is the grinding and the beating. The two kinds of meat should be put through a grinder *three* times, preferably at home rather than by the butcher, until fine and light. Add the flour and milk, and then you beat and you beat and then beat some more until you are exhausted and the batter is light, smooth, and fluffy. Scoop up a tablespoonful and form with your hand into an oval-shaped ball. Sauté in butter over a low flame for about 15 minutes, turning now and then to get an even brown. Serve with boiled potatoes and browned butter. Serves 4.

Italian potato, egg, and cheese dish

TIME: 1½ HOURS

For a late supper, luncheon, or even for Sunday breakfast, if the salad is omitted.

Menu: ITALIAN POTATO, EGG, AND CHEESE DISH
ROUMANIAN GREEN PEPPER SALAD (see page 21)
BREAD STICKS
FRESH CHERRIES AND PEARS
COFFEE

ITALIAN POTATO, EGG, AND CHEESE DISH:

3 medium-sized potatoes, boiled, peeled, and cut in thick slices
1 lump of Mozzarella cheese, cut in thin slices
Salt and pepper
⅓ cup grated Parmesan cheese
⅓ cup finely chopped parsley
¼ cup melted butter
4 eggs

Put a layer of the sliced potatoes in the bottom of a shallow, buttered casserole. Cover with slices of Mozzarella, sprinkle with salt and pepper, and then the grated cheese and parsley. Repeat the layers in this way until all ingredients are used. The casserole should be large enough in diameter so that there are only 2 or 3 layers. Pour the melted butter over all and carefully break the four eggs on top. Bake in a 350° oven 20 minutes or until the eggs are set and the cheese is melted. Serves 4.

Baked stuffed tufoli (Italian)

TIME: PRACTICALLY ALL DAY

Tufoli is the pasta in a large tube practically begging to be stuffed. As far as I know it always is, sometimes with mashed meat balls, other times with this more delicate stuffing of ricotta (the Italian cheese somewhat like cottage cheese but with a more subtle flavor), grated Parmesan, eggs, and parsley. However, this recipe has everything. The meat balls are broken into the sauce.

Menu: BAKED STUFFED TUFOLI
        MIXED GREEN SALAD, FRENCH DRESSING (2 PARTS OLIVE
          OIL, 1 PART VINEGAR, SALT AND PEPPER)
        FRENCH OR ITALIAN BREAD
        FRESH PEACHES IN RED WINE
        COFFEE

BAKED STUFFED TUFOLI:

Make Italian meat balls with tomato sauce according to recipe on page 60.

> 1 pound tufoli
> 1 pound ricotta
> ⅓ cup grated Parmesan cheese
> 2 eggs
> 3 tablespoons chopped parsley
> Salt and pepper
> More grated Parmesan and a lump Mozzarella

Cook the tufoli in a large pan of rapidly boiling salted water until tender but not squishy. Drain. Make stuffing by blending thoroughly the ricotta, Parmesan cheese, eggs, parsley, salt and pepper. An electric beater may be used for this. Stuff the tufoli, using a teaspoon. Put a layer of the stuffed tufoli in the bottom of a large casserole, crumble the meat balls over the top, cover with tomato sauce, and sprinkle generously with more Parmesan cheese. Cover this with thin slices of Mozzarella. Repeat the layers until all the ingredients are used. There should be 2 or 3 layers. Use plenty of sauce or it will get dry. Bake at 350° for 1 hour. Serves 6 to 8.

Portuguese red bean soup

TIME: 12 TO 24 HOURS WITH DRIED BEANS, 3 HOURS WITH CANNED

This soup comes from Portugal by way of the fishermen on Cape Cod. Mostly they cook here the same dishes they always cooked in the old country.

Menu: PORTUGUESE RED BEAN SOUP
      HOT CORN BREAD
      WATER-CRESS SALAD WITH FRENCH DRESSING (2 PARTS OLIVE OIL, 1 PART GARLIC VINEGAR, SALT AND PEPPER)
      LIME CHIFFON PIE
      COFFEE

PORTUGUESE RED BEAN SOUP:

1 cup uncooked red kidney beans, soaked overnight, or 2 cans kidney beans, drained
3 medium-sized onions, sliced
4 tablespoons bacon fat
2 cloves garlic, minced
6 medium-sized potatoes, peeled and diced
3 or 4 bay leaves
1 tablespoon allspice
1 can Italian tomato paste
Salt and pepper

Simmer the kidney beans until tender. Sauté the onions in the bacon fat. Boil the potatoes and when about half done add to the undrained potatoes the sautéed onions and garlic, beans, bay leaves, allspice, tomato paste, salt and pepper. Add water if necessary. This should be a good, sloshy consistency. Let it simmer for about 3 hours before serving. Serves 4 to 6 generously.

Swiss spinach pie

TIME: 1 HOUR

Now the Swiss really like pie and are apt to have in one meal a spinach or cheese pie along with a fruit pie, such as a greengage plum tart. They eat them together, a bit of spinach or cheese, a bit of plum, and so on, along with lots of good strong coffee. For Americans who worry about their waistlines and who do not have their mountains quite so handy for climbing and working off their extra weight a lighter menu is suggested.

Menu: MITITEI (see page 80)
SWISS SPINACH PIE
HOT ROLLS
FRESH STRAWBERRIES, CRÈME CHANTILLY (DELICATE BUT
TANGY SWEDISH CREAM CHEESE AVAILABLE HERE IN
MANY PLACES)

SWISS SPINACH PIE:
3 pounds raw spinach, finely chopped, or 2 packages chopped frozen
1 9-inch pie shell
Salt and pepper
5 strips bacon

Salt the spinach to get the bitter black juice out and squeeze dry. Pile the pie shell with the spinach and sprinkle with the salt and pepper, preferably freshly ground. Cover with bacon strips and bake in a 400° oven about 15 minutes (or until crust is brown). Serves 4.

Spaghetti with clams and diced raw ham (Italian)

TIME: 45 MINUTES

To the American mind spaghetti is meat balls with tomato sauce, but in Italy the many, many shapes of pasta are anointed with almost as many different sauces. They are usually good, and often as simple as this.

Menu: SPAGHETTI WITH CLAMS AND DICED RAW HAM
ROUMANIAN CUCUMBER SALAD (see page 159)
FRENCH OR ITALIAN BREAD
RHUBARB BAKED WITH STRAWBERRIES, AND THIN CRISP
GINGER COOKIES
COFFEE

SPAGHETTI WITH CLAMS AND DICED RAW HAM:
¼ pound diced raw ham
2 tablespoons lemon juice
1 pint fresh-shucked clams, chopped, or 1 can minced clams and the juice
1 pound pasta (the shell-shaped would be pretty in this), cooked in rapidly boiling salted water until tender but not mushy
1 stick (¼ pound) unsalted butter

Cook the ham in the butter until frizzled. Add the lemon juice and clams. Simmer slowly for about 5 minutes. Add a little salt if needed, but the ham and clams are both salty. Pour over the cooked pasta, swish around, and serve immediately. Serves 4.

Red beans and rice

TIME: 12 HOURS WITH DRIED BEANS, 30 MINUTES WITH CANNED BEANS

All around the Caribbean rice is cooked with beans, usually red, though here and there the beans are black and in a few places not beans but dried green peas are used. The protein and meaty consistency of the dried legumes combine very pleasingly with the rice and whatever is in the larder or the mood of the moment suggests. This is a frugal one-dish meal, even though more lavish accompaniments are suggested in the menu.

Menu: BROILED HAM
      RED BEANS AND RICE
      SALAD OF MIXED GREENS WITH THIN SLICES OF AVOCADO,
         GRAPEFRUIT SEGMENTS, AND FRENCH DRESSING (2 PARTS
         OLIVE OIL, 1 PART VINEGAR, SALT AND PEPPER)
      LIME ICE
      MACAROONS
      COFFEE

RED BEANS AND RICE:

    ¼ *pound salt pork, diced*
    1 large onion, chopped fine
    2 cans red kidney beans, drained, or 1 pound dried soaked
       overnight and simmered until tender
    1½ cups long-grained rice

Sauté the salt pork, add the onion, cook until the onion is pale yellow but still crisp. Add the beans and transfer to a deep saucepan. Add the rice, 3 cups water, 2 teaspoons salt and bring to a boil. Cover tightly, turn heat very low, and cook for about 20 minutes before removing cover to taste for doneness. It is finished when the rice is dry and fluffy.

In the West Indies coconut milk is often used as the liquid. The meat of the coconut is grated into a cup of boiling water and let stand. The liquid then squeezed out becomes coconut milk. This is work, but tastes so good that it is worth the unaccustomed bother. Serves 4.

Cottage cheese cakes with sour cream (sirniki—Russian)

TIME: 45 MINUTES

This Russian dish, served all the year, is a special favorite for lunch and for Lent.

Menu: SIRNIKI

COLD COOKED GLOBE ARTICHOKES WITH A BOWL OF HEAVILY SALTED AND PEPPERED OLIVE OIL TO DIP THE LEAVES IN

STEWED RHUBARB WITH STRAWBERRIES

COFFEE

SIRNIKI:

3 cups pot cheese (if cottage cheese is used it must be drained for several hours)
2 eggs, slightly beaten
2 tablespoons sour cream
⅔ cup sifted flour
Salt
More flour
¼ cup (½ stick) butter
Sour cream

Mix the pot cheese, eggs, sour cream, salt, and flour. Make into balls about the size of a golf ball and pat down until they are about ¾ inch thick. Dust with more flour and sauté until brown in the hot butter. Drain on paper and serve with a bowl of sour cream that has been warmed but not allowed to boil (boiling doesn't harm it, but separates the cream unaesthetically). Serves 4.

Yoghurt

TIME: ALL DAY

Long ago, in the days before refrigeration and pasteurization, there were only two ways to keep milk, both of them delicious: one, a solid (cheese), for a comparatively long time, and one (semi-liquid) for a comparatively brief period. The semi-liquid one is called variously yoghurt (spelled variously too), leben, matzoon, filbunke, and so on, depending upon the country in which it is made. For years it was eaten or drunk because it kept better than fresh milk and because it tasted good with so many foods. It still does and is more rewarding to make than to buy. It is also good for you, a good point to keep in mind but rather a dull one to discuss very often.

Bring a quart of milk to a boil, lower the flame, and let it simmer just under the boiling point for about 15 minutes. Remove from the fire and allow to cool for about 10 minutes. The commercial yoghurt is used for a starter the first time—use some of your own the next time, but buy a little fresh from time to time (this bacillus can get very tired). Put 3 tablespoons yoghurt starter in a cup and add about ½ cup of the warmed milk. Test the rest of the milk with your little finger; if lukewarm, add the yoghurt mixture and mix slowly. Pour into a bowl and cover. Place the bowl in a moderately warm place where there isn't a draft, such as in an unheated oven or in a closet, and an Armenian friend of mine says that you should wrap it in your grandmother's shawl. It will set in about 4 to 6 hours. When firm put bowl into the refrigerator. Serve cold. Larger or smaller quantities may be made by doubling or halving these proportions. Serve over chopped cucumbers or a combination of chopped cucumbers, onions, or radishes, over hot baked *kasha,* or present it for dessert the way they do at the Gripsholm Restaurant in New York. The yoghurt, or *filbunke,* as the Swedish call it, is served in a bowl and you are passed a tray with about a half-dozen accompaniments to sprinkle on it much in the same way the accompaniments to a curry are served. The ones served with filbunke are apt to be pumpernickel crumbs, finely chopped nuts, brown sugar, cinnamon, and nutmeg.

Tempura (Japanese)

TIME: 1¼ HOURS

Tempura, as served in Japanese-American restaurants, is a very fine version of batter-fried shrimp. Authentically made, according to a Japanese artist, an artist in the kitchen, too, tempura is deep-fried bits of this and that, much like the Italian *fritto misto*. The Japanese being the people they are, with a feeling for decoration, each food is cut in a pretty design.

Menu: TEMPURA
> SALAD: WATER CRESS WITH SLICED RAW MUSHROOM CAPS MARINATED IN FRENCH DRESSING (2 PARTS OLIVE OIL, 1 PART LEMON JUICE, SALT AND PEPPER)
> LEMON SHERBET WITH BLACK BING CHERRIES ON TOP
> TEA

TEMPURA:

The amounts will vary according to the occasion.

> *Sweet potatoes, peeled and cut in diagonal slices ½ inch thick*
>
> *Shrimp, peeled and split part way, butterfly-fashion, leaving the tail on*
>
> *Seasonal vegetables cut decoratively (carrots, in long strips, string beans cut slantwise, green onions cut in 3-inch pieces, and so on)*
>
> *Chrysanthemum leaves (these are pretty and traditional, but be sure they have not been sprayed with a poison)*
>
> *Crisp parsley in clumps*

Batter:

> *Whole egg, slightly beaten*
> *Flour*
> *Pinch baking powder*
> *Salt and pepper*

Sauce:

> *Soy sauce*
> *Grated white radish (a nice sharp accent when obtainable)*
> *Vegetable oil for deep frying*

After the vegetables have been prepared, make a batter by mixing the egg with a little flour, baking powder, salt and pepper, and enough water to make it about as thin as pancake batter or heavy cream. Dip the vegetables and shrimp into the batter and fry a few at a time in the oil, which has been heated to 345° to 355°, or hot enough to brown 1-inch cube of day-old bread in 65 seconds. Cook until brown. Serve with tiny bowls of soy sauce mixed with the grated white radish.

Armenian baked clams or mussels

TIME: 1¾ HOURS

Somehow mussels would seem more authentic for this dish, but the Armenian friend who gave me the recipe uses clams. Either way is good.

Menu: ARMENIAN BAKED CLAMS OR MUSSELS
      CAPELLINI (see page 183)
      GREEN PEPPER SALAD (see page 21)
      COFFEE

ARMENIAN BAKED CLAMS OR MUSSELS:
2 dozen clams or mussels
2 cups bread crumbs
⅓ cup finely chopped parsley
2 tablespoons lemon juice
1 medium-sized onion, chopped fine

Scrub the clams or mussels thoroughly. Put in a roasting pan, and then in a 300° oven for 2 or 3 minutes or until the shells open. Remove immediately from the oven and remove the clams or mussels from the shells, saving and straining the juice in the pan through a piece of cheesecloth. There is apt to be a bit of sand no matter how well you wash them. Chop the clams or mussels, coarsely mix with the bread crumbs, parsley, lemon juice, and onion. Fill the shells with this stuffing, force the shells together, and tie with a string. Bake about 1 hour in a 350° oven. Remove the string before serving the clams or mussels. Serves 4.

Capellini (Italian)

TIME: 30 MINUTES

This pasta is one of the finest of all in size. In fact the name means fine hair. It takes about 1 minute to cook. Longer than that, it becomes squashy. In Italy this is traditionally served on Christmas Eve with broiled eel and steamed escarole stuffed with raisins and pignolias, but it is good any time of the year, with untraditional and un-Italian accompaniments.

Menu: CANADIAN BACON, BAKED WHOLE AND BASTED WITH MUS-
CATEL WINE
CAPELLINI
RAW SPINACH SALAD WITH TOMATO DRESSING (BLEND 1
TABLESPOON TOMATO CATCHUP, 3 TABLESPOONS OLIVE
OIL, 1 TABLESPOON VINEGAR, SALT AND PEPPER)
FRESH PLUMS WITH CRÈME CHANTILLY (THE TANGY
SWEDISH CREAM CHEESE)
COFFEE

CAPELLINI:

3 whole cloves garlic
¼ cup olive oil
Salt and pepper
1 pound capellini or other very fine pasta
½ cup coarsely chopped walnuts

Heat the garlic, salt and pepper in the olive oil. Cook the pasta in rapidly boiling salted water until tender. Drain. Remove the garlic from the olive oil. Pour the olive oil over the hot pasta and toss with a fork and spoon until each strand is coated with the seasoned oil. Sprinkle with the chopped walnuts and serve immediately. Serves 4 generously.

Stuffed grape leaves (Armenian)

TIME: 1 HOUR

This recipe always sounds very strange to an American the first time he hears about it. In most European countries people mix chopped meat with rice and roll it up in a leaf of some kind. The grape leaves may be bought in cans at Armenian or Greek groceries and give the mixture a delicate flavor. Fresh ones, dropped for a minute in boiling water to make them pliable, may be used.

Menu: STUFFED GRAPE LEAVES
GREEN PEPPER SALAD (see page 21)
FRENCH BREAD
COFFEE ICE CREAM WITH BITTER-CHOCOLATE SAUCE
COFFEE

STUFFED GRAPE LEAVES:

1 pound lean shoulder lamb, ground
¼ cup uncooked rice
1 tablespoon chopped fresh dill, or 1 teaspoon dried
Juice ¼ lemon
½ cup finely chopped parsley
1 small onion, chopped fine
1 can grape leaves, rinsed and patted dry
1 can Italian tomato paste
1 can tomato juice (1 pint 2 ounces)

Mix the lamb, rice, dill, lemon juice, parsley, and onion together. Put a tablespoon of the mixture on each leaf, vein side up, and roll up tightly. Put in a large pot, weight the grape leaves down with a plate to keep them closed or skewer them with toothpicks. Add the tomato paste diluted with tomato juice. Cover and simmer for 45 minutes. Serve in the sauce. Serves 6 generously.

Fancy pilau, Persian version

TIME: 12 HOURS

The Persians, like all from the Far and Near East, cook rice lovingly and well day in and day out. However, for special occasions they cook it in a special way, as in this recipe.

Menu: ROAST LAMB

DEEP-FRIED GREEN BEANS (DIP COOKED BEANS IN A THIN BATTER AND FRY IN DEEP FAT UNTIL CRISP)

FANCY PILAU

BEET RELISH (CHOPPED COOKED BEETS, OLIVE OIL, FINELY CHOPPED PARSLEY, MINCED GARLIC, SALT)

PIDEH, THE ARMENIAN BREAD, OR, MORE CONVENIENTLY, FRENCH BREAD

HOT BROILED GRAPEFRUIT

COFFEE

FANCY PILAU:

1 pound long-grained rice, or riza sadirie (the fancy Persian variety)

3 tablespoons butter

3 medium-sized potatoes, peeled and sliced thin

⅓ cup raisins, plumped in water

⅛ teaspoon saffron, soaked in hot water

Soak the rice overnight in cold water (these are Persian instructions). Rinse it well and start to boil it in a large amount of salted cold water. When tender but still firm, strain, rinse with cold water to firm and separate. Put a lump of butter in a shallow baking pan or casserole, cover the bottom with the slices of raw potatoes. Dot with a few lumps of butter. Spread the rice evenly over the butter and potatoes. Sprinkle with the raisins and saffron water. Add the melted butter over the rice. Cover and steam in the oven about 15 minutes at what my Persian friend calls half blast and I call 350° to 375° oven. Shake gently from side to side and let stand 10 minutes. Put in serving dish, discarding the potatoes. Serve with stewed prunes on the side. Serves 6 to 8 Americans, 4 Persians.

185

Scottish tripe and onions (poor man's oysters)

TIME: 4 HOURS

When I was writing a column on a large city newspaper, I had frequent talks with a dour but beloved city editor. When there was a lull in City Hall news, school news, and no new wreck or murder, he would come to my desk, pull up a chair, and talk happily about food, a subject he much preferred to those in his own work routine. His wife was Scottish and he liked many dishes from that country, despite their dismal reputation. This one, which he and his wife served for late Sunday morning breakfasts, he especially liked, and so did I after I had tried it. It seems to have a slight oysterish flavor, but perhaps it is only the texture that makes one think so. It is pleasing for the first meal after a long, long night of rest. Pressure cooking has no ill-effects on the texture of the tripe and shortens the cooking time considerably.

Menu: BROILED GRAPEFRUIT HALVES, SERVED WARM
SCOTTISH TRIPE AND ONIONS, ON TOAST OR BISCUITS (UN-
DOUBTEDLY AN AMERICAN MODIFICATION—IT SHOULD
PROBABLY BE BANNOCKS OR SOME SUCH TYPICALLY
SCOTTISH BREAD)
BACON BISCUITS (ANY GOOD DROPPED OR ROLLED BISCUIT
WITH BITS OF COOKED BACON THROUGHOUT)
COFFEE

SCOTTISH TRIPE AND ONIONS:

1 pound cleaned honeycomb tripe, cut in 2-inch squares
1 pint milk
3 medium-sized onions, peeled and sliced thin
3 tablespoons butter
3 tablespoons flour
1 pint more milk
Salt and lots of freshly ground black pepper
Hot biscuits or toast

Put the tripe in cold water, bring to a boil, drain, and throw away that water. Cover with the milk and 2 cups fresh water, add the onions and simmer for 3 hours, or cook under pressure for 1. (Naturally you should cook this the night before and let it sit in the milk overnight, unless you are a very early riser.) Make a sauce by melting the butter, blending in the flour, and cooking for 5 minutes or more until the floury taste is gone. Add the salt and pepper and stir in 2 cups fresh milk (discard the milk the tripe was cooked in) gradually, cooking until thick and smooth. Add the drained tripe and onions. Serves 4.

Roumanian meat cakes (chiftele marinate)

TIME: 2 HOURS

As I have been saying, every country cooks its chopped meat just a little differently and extremely well.

Menu: CHIFTELE MARINATE
       BAKED POTATOES
       WATER CRESS WITH FRENCH DRESSING (2 PARTS OLIVE
          OIL, 1 PART WINE VINEGAR, SALT AND PEPPER)
       WINE JELLY
       COFFEE

CHIFTELE MARINATE:
    2 pounds lean beef
    ½ pound lean pork
    (both ground together twice by the butcher)
    3 or 4 slices bread, crust cut off and soaked in water, then
       squeezed out
    Salt and pepper
    ⅓ cup finely chopped parsley
    2 eggs
    1 clove garlic, chopped fine
    Flour
    1 stick butter (¼ pound), or ½ cup oil

Sauce:
    3 large onions, chopped fine
    6 bay leaves
    24 peppercorns
    1 can bouillon or 1 bouillon cube dissolved in 1 cup water
    1 can (8 ounces) tomato sauce
    ½ large can Italian plum tomatoes

Mix the ingredients for the meat cakes, dust with flour, sauté slowly in the butter or oil. Remove from the skillet. In the fat left in the pan sauté the onions until soft and slightly golden, add the bay leaves, peppercorns, bouillon, tomato sauce, tomatoes and simmer for 1 hour. Add the meat cakes. Cook 30 to 45 minutes longer. These meat cakes are often served just sautéed with no sauce, also they may be made very small, just slightly larger than marbles, sautéed and served hot as cocktail bites. Obviously this is an American adaptation. This amount will make a large number of hot hors d'oeuvres, but in my experience there are never any left over.

Frittata di zucchini (Italian)

TIME: 35 MINUTES

This is one of the pleasing ways in which Italians give substance to an egg dish. It makes a good, light, improvised meal for lunch, for a late supper, or for those sudden and unscheduled hungers.

Menu: FRITTATA DI ZUCCHINI
   SALADE NIÇOISE (see page 70)
   FRENCH OR ITALIAN BREAD
   CHERRY TARTS
   COFFEE

FRITTATA DI ZUCCHINI:
   3 tablespoons olive oil
   1 medium-sized zucchini, sliced thin but not peeled
   6 eggs, beaten slightly
   Salt and pepper

Heat the oil in a skillet and sauté the zucchini briefly, until the rawness is gone but it is still slightly crisp. Pour the eggs, beaten with ⅓ cup water, salt and pepper over the zucchini. Cook over a low heat until the eggs are done, stirring all the while. Serves 3.

Yorkshire pudding (English)

TIME: 50 MINUTES

The old baronial days in England are gone and not likely to return, but Yorkshire pudding still goes on with smaller roasts. It's true most people do not have a hand-turned spit and a pan to collect the juices, but the pan underneath an electric rotisserie, which many do have, will hold some of the juices, or drippings. Spoon the drippings in the bottom of a square Mexican casserole, which is the traditional shape, if most unauthentic.

Menu: ROAST BEEF OR STEAK
       YORKSHIRE PUDDING
       WATER CRESS IN A BOWL, NO DRESSING
       PLUM TART
       COFFEE

YORKSHIRE PUDDING:
> *2 eggs*
> *1 cup milk*
> *1 cup flour*
> *Pinch salt*
> *Meat drippings*

Beat the eggs with the milk and add the flour, which has been sifted with the salt. Beat until blended. Pour the drippings into a square casserole, and then pour the batter over that. The batter should be about ½ inch deep. Bake in a 450° oven until brown and puffy, which should take about ½ hour. (This time it is especially important to preheat the oven.) Serve cut in squares. Serves 4 to 6.

Nassi goreng (Indonesian)

TIME: 45 MINUTES

This is a good mishmash dish made with whatever colorful and flavorful bits of this and that are in the refrigerator, added to curried fried rice. In Holland House in New York this is always topped with a wedge of cucumber, cut the length of the cucumber, and a fried egg.

Menu: NASSI GORENG
      BELGIAN TOMATO SALAD (see page 98)
      HOT POPPY-SEED ROLLS
      CHEESECAKE
      COFFEE

NASSI GORENG:

⅓ cup butter
2 tablespoons curry powder
1 cup uncooked rice
1 small onion, chopped fine
Salt and pepper
2 cups chicken broth
1 buffet-size can shrimp, cleaned
1 buffet-size can hearts of artichoke drained
1 slice diced cooked ham

Melt the butter, add the curry powder, stir until smooth. Add the rice and cook that over a low flame until it is well coated with the spicy blend. Add the onion, salt and pepper. Cook until the onion is almost tender. Add the chicken broth. Bring to a boil, cover, and cook over very low heat for about 15 minutes. Remove the cover, add the shrimp, hearts of artichoke, and ham and simmer for about 5 to 10 minutes, long enough for the flavors to get well acquainted. Serves 4.

Bourride (French)

TIME: 1 HOUR

To my admittedly prejudiced mind this is the best of all fish soups, deceptively bland and unexpectedly filling. Its creamy texture makes it seem a delicate prelude to a meal, but with bread, crisp French-fried zucchini and salad, it is a meal for all but the very hearty eaters.

Menu: BOURRIDE
FRENCH BREAD
FRENCH-FRIED ZUCCHINI
TOSSED GREEN SALAD, WITH FRENCH DRESSING (2 PARTS OLIVE OIL, 1 PART VINEGAR, SALT AND PEPPER)
FRESH BLACK BING CHERRIES
COFFEE

BOURRIDE:

2 pounds fish (fresh), cut in pieces
Court bouillon (simmer in 1 quart water: 1 carrot chopped, 1 onion chopped, 1 stalk celery chopped, 1 sprig parsley minced, 1 bay leaf, 6 or 8 peppercorns, mushroom peelings, ¼ cup white wine or 2 tablespoons vinegar, for 30 minutes. Strain.)
Aoli (3 cloves garlic, mashed fine. Blend with 1 egg and add 1 cup olive oil, teaspoon by teaspoon, beating until thick and smooth. Thin with 1 tablespoon lemon juice, add salt and pepper, or make in the electric blender, using directions for mayonnaise.)
Fried croutons

Poach the fish in the strained court bouillon for about 10 minutes, or until the fish is white and opaque. Remove half the pieces of fish and mash the others in the broth to get as much of the essence as possible. Strain and let liquid cool slightly. Put the aoli in the top of a double boiler and add the warm fish broth bit by bit, stirring until creamy and thick. Do not cook. Serve in bowls with a few pieces of fish and a few croutons in each. Serves 4.

Zwiebelküchen—Swiss or German onion pie

TIME: 1¼ HOURS

Serve this proudly as a main dish for a light meal, a lunch, or Sunday-night supper. There are many versions, all good. The French use cheese with the eggs instead of sour cream and caraway seed. Europeans are so much better than we are at giving each vegetable its turn for attention.

Menu: ZWIEBELKÜCHEN

> CAESAR SALAD (TORN ROMAINE OR ESCAROLE, WITH A CRUMBLED WEDGE OF ROQUEFORT CHEESE, ½ CUP FRESHLY GRATED PARMESAN CHEESE; 2 PARTS OLIVE OIL, 1 PART LEMON JUICE, SALT AND PEPPER, A DASH WORCESTERSHIRE SAUCE; CROUTONS, TOSSED IN ½ CUP OLIVE OIL CONTAINING 1 CLOVE GARLIC. RAW EGG IS USUAL BUT NOT ESSENTIAL.)
>
> GARLIC BREAD
>
> KISSEL (CRANBERRY JUICE SWEETENED, THICKENED SLIGHTLY WITH CORNSTARCH. CHILL AND SERVE WITH CREAM.)
>
> COFFEE

ZWIEBELKÜCHEN:

> *8 to 10 large onions, sliced thin*
> *¼ cup butter*
> *4 tablespoons flour*
> *1 cup sour cream*
> *2 eggs*
> *Salt*
> *1 tablespoon caraway seed*
> *Pie crust for 9-inch pie*

Sauté the onions in the butter until tender and glossy but not brown. Remove from heat. In a bowl mix the flour slowly with the sour cream, beaten eggs, salt, and caraway seed. Add the onions and stir well. Turn into the pie crust in a pie tin. Bake in a hot oven, 450°, for 10 minutes, reduce heat to 300° and bake ½ hour more or until crust is light brown. Two or three pieces of finely diced bacon may be put in the pie crust first. Serves 4.

Moules marinière—French

TIME: 1 HOUR

No one in America is born loving mussels, a delight to palate and eye, according to the sad report of the Fishery Council of New York. Mussel eaters are foreign-born, learn to like them in foreign restaurants here or abroad, or else they learn to like them in the home of foreign-born friends. Mussels are good in the fine, simple peasant dishes and in gourmet concoctions. Cleaning them is a bit of bother, but the final appearance of the gleaming black shells with the pale orange flesh glowing in the opalescent lining is ample reward. The French and the Italians admire them so much that shells and all are served in most dishes, the shell making a beautiful scoop for the juices in the dish.

Menu: MOULES MARINIÈRE
SALAD: MIXED GREENS WITH FRENCH DRESSING (2 PARTS OLIVE OIL, 1 PART TARRAGON VINEGAR, SALT AND PEPPER)
LOTS OF FRENCH BREAD FOR MOPPING UP JUICES
FRESH RHUBARB PIE
COFFEE

MOULES MARINIÈRE:
  4 pounds mussels
  ½ cup dry white wine
  1 stalk celery
  1 small onion, chopped
  Salt and pepper
  ¼ cup melted butter

Let cold water run over the mussels for ½ hour, then plunge into lukewarm water for about 2 minutes. They will open and close and wash themselves. Throw away any that float on top. Scrub the shells with a stiff brush until they are smooth and gleaming. Put them in a saucepan with the wine, celery, onion, salt and pepper. Cover and steam about 5 minutes until the shells are open. Remove the mussels from the broth and pull off the top shell. Keep warm. Put in a deep tureen or in individual deep, warm soup bowls. Strain the broth, mix with the melted butter, and pour over the mussels. This is one of the dishes you may eat almost any way. You may use one of the shells as a scoop or, more genteelly, an oyster fork and soupspoon, but don't be too finicky to mop up the juices with bread. The old Lafayette Hotel in New York used to make a version of Moules Marinière with a few spoonfuls of hollandaise stirred into the juice, making it almost moules Poulette. Serves 4.

Tacos (Mexican)

TIME: 1½ HOURS

This is the Mexican equivalent of a sandwich and like much Mexican food is highly seasoned. It is best when approaching Mexican food for the first time to season gently until your taste buds become used to these fiery foods. Also beer or milk should be drunk with it to ameliorate the hotness. Tom Gullette, who grew up in Texas and wandered back and forth over the border, says that tortillas taste much the best when made by a beautiful and very young Mexican girl whose hands have not been washed very recently. However, he has been known, when far away, to buy them from a Mexican restaurant or store or else, when the blue corn meal that is traditional was obtainable, to make them himself with clean hands, being neither very young nor very beautiful, using the same proportions as in a *crêpes Suzette* recipe.

Menu: TACOS   BEER
        RHUBARB PIE
        COFFEE

TACOS:

> 1 medium-sized onion, chopped
> 1 fat clove garlic, minced
> Bacon fat
> 1 pound ground beef
> Chile powder (5 or 6 chile pods well crumbled for those who are used to it)
> Lettuce
> Tomatoes
> 1 dozen tortillas
> Lard

Cook the onion and garlic in the bacon fat until pale yellow. Add the beef to the onion and garlic and cook slowly until browned, stirring from time to time. Add the chile and cook until the flavors are well mingled. Sauté the tortillas in lard on both sides. Put a large spoonful on each tortilla. Fold in half with some shredded lettuce in one end and a wedge of tomato in the other for freshness and authenticity. Serves 4 for lunch or supper.

Japanese soup

TIME: 30 MINUTES

The prettiest of all foods I have seen come from two countries wide apart geographically and sociologically—Japan and Denmark. Any dish from these two countries is a beautiful thing to look at as well as to eat. Food from other countries is different and delicious, but somehow not quite so aesthetically presented. It is silly to go on about a simple broth no matter how delicate the flavor. This thin clear broth, served in plain bowls, preferably black lacquer, is exquisite with its thin slivers of vegetables.

Menu: JAPANESE SOUP
TEMPURA (see page 180)
HOT COOKED RICE WITH SOY SAUCE
BOWL OF SLICED CUCUMBERS IN ICE WATER WITH FINELY
CHOPPED MINT (REMOVE THE CRISP SLICES WITH FORK
OR FINGERS)
COFFEE ICE CREAM WITH CHOCOLATE BITS
TEA

JAPANESE SOUP:
5 uncooked shrimp, peeled and black vein removed
Few slivers onion
Few slivers carrot with serrated edges
1 stalk celery
Salt and pinch sugar
Dash soy sauce

Simmer the shrimp in 4 cups water until pink. Add the slivers of onion, carrot, celery, salt and sugar, soy sauce. Simmer 15 minutes, remove the celery and discard. Put into small, warm bowls and add a thin piece of lemon peel, a dash of lemon juice, and a crisp sprig of parsley to each bowl. For a richer soup, but one not so clear or pretty, add one well-beaten egg to the soup before pouring into the bowls. Serves 4.

Italian codfish with green peppers and onions

TIME: 3 HOURS, INCLUDING SOAKING TIME

This is one of the more pleasing ways of cooking the salt codfish available to inlanders almost anywhere, and cooked by Southern Europeans often in preference to their plentiful fresh fish.

Menu: ITALIAN CODFISH WITH GREEN PEPPERS AND ONIONS
PRESSED CUCUMBER SALAD (see menu, page 168)
FRENCH OR ITALIAN BREAD
FRESH BLUEBERRY PIE
COFFEE

ITALIAN CODFISH WITH GREEN PEPPERS AND ONIONS:
½ cup olive oil
1½ pounds salt codfish, soaked for several hours, drained and cut into 2- or 3-inch squares
5 green peppers, tops and seeds removed and cut into thick slices
3 medium-sized onions, peeled and cut into thick slices
⅓ cup finely chopped parsley
Salt and pepper

In a large skillet heat the olive oil and sauté the codfish, peppers, and onion together, stirring frequently. Before serving drain if necessary, sprinkle with the chopped parsley, salt and pepper. Serves 4.

Lancashire hot pot (English)

TIME: 3½ HOURS

In this particular part of England the hot pot, stew by another name, is always cooked in a pot similar to our New England bean pot or the French *marmite*.

Menu: LANCASHIRE HOT POT
       SALAD: SLICED TOMATOES WITH FRENCH DRESSING (2 PARTS OLIVE OIL, 1 PART VINEGAR, SALT AND PEPPER)
       TOASTED ENGLISH MUFFINS
       CHILLED PEARS WITH A SAUCE OF MELTED RASPBERRY JAM
       COFFEE

LANCASHIRE HOT POT:
    6 large potatoes, peeled and sliced thick
    4 large carrots, scraped and sliced
    4 large onions, peeled and sliced
    4 shoulder lamb or mutton chops
    Salt and pepper
    2 cups beef bouillon or 2 cubes dissolved in 2 cups water, or 2 cups leftover gravy

In a deep, deep casserole, French marmite, or bean pot put a layer of the sliced potatoes, a layer of carrots, and one of onions. Then put in the chops, season with salt and pepper gently (the bouillon has some), and repeat the layers of vegetables, being careful to end up with potatoes on top. Pour the bouillon in, cover, and cook slowly either on top of the stove or in the oven for about 3 hours, removing the lid for the last hour to brown the potatoes. Serves 4.

Yellow pea soup (gule aerter—Danish)

TIME: 2½ TO 3 HOURS

Soup in Denmark, particularly in the winter, is not a meager come-on for the rest of the meal. It is a sturdy and sustaining fare for a cold winter night. In this one, which is much like the Swedish *ärter med fläsk* and the French-Canadian *Habitant* soup, the Danes serve diced boiled potatoes in the soup. The pork is sliced and served on a separate plate with the soup or else in the tureen; either is traditional. This soup practically demands a good tureen or large, deep casserole for the proper presentation.

Menu: GULE AERTER
      DILL PICKLES
      THIN PANCAKES WITH LINGONBERRIES (THE SCANDINAVIAN
        CRANBERRY)
      COFFEE

GULE AERTER:
> *1 pound dried peas, preferably the yellow, though the green will do*
> *2 pounds salt pork, in one piece (this is a lavish version— the pork may be halved for frugality)*
> *Chopped celery leaves*
> *2 leeks, or 1 large onion, quartered*
> *½ teaspoon thyme*
> *Salt and pepper*
> *3 boiled potatoes, peeled and diced*

Bring all the ingredients, covered with water, to a vigorous boil. Cook this way for about an hour. Most of the skins will come off the peas in the boiling. Skim them off the top, drain the peas, reserving the liquid. Slice the pork and keep warm. Press the peas through a sieve or ricer and mix with the liquid. Add the boiled potatoes and pour into one tureen with the pork and serve the sliced pork in a warm platter on the side. Serves 6 to 8.

A rich minestrone (Italian)

TIME: 3 TO 4 HOURS

The pot that simmers on the back of most Italian stoves, day in and day out, usually contains minestrone (the *pot-au-feu* is on the French stoves), the basic meal-in-itself soup of these people.

Menu: MINESTRONE
ARTICHOKES WITH ONION AND DILL (see page 49)
ITALIAN BREAD
RHUBARB BREAD PUDDING
COFFEE

MINESTRONE:

½ *pound fat back, chopped finely*
2 *cloves garlic, peeled and minced*
3 *large onions, chopped*
4 *carrots, scraped and sliced*
2 *stalks celery, chopped fine*
⅓ *cup finely chopped parsley*
4 *medium-sized tomatoes, skinned and seeded, or 1 large can, strained*
Salt and pepper
Orégano
1 *cup string beans, fresh or frozen, broken into pieces*
1 *cup peas*
1 *cup fresh lima beans*
½ *medium-sized head cabbage, cut in wedges*
4 *potatoes, peeled and cut in quarters*
1 *cup canned ceci (garbanzas or chick-peas), soaked, cooked, and drained*
1 *handful ditalini or any other small-sized or fine pasta*

Cook the fat back (salt pork without even a streak of lean) slowly in a skillet. Add the garlic and onions and sauté until pale yellow. Put in a heavy soup kettle or Dutch oven with the carrots, celery, parsley, and tomatoes. Add 2 quarts water and simmer 1½ to 2 hours. Add the rest of the vegetables and simmer for 1 hour more. About 10 minutes before you plan to serve, add the ditalini. In Northern Italy a spoonful of *pesto* is added to each bowl of soup. This is made by mixing 3 cloves garlic mashed to a paste, preferably in a mortar, with 2 tablespoons chopped fresh basil, 2 tablespoons freshly grated Parmesan cheese, 2 tablespoons olive oil, and 1 tablespoon butter, preferably unsalted. Blend well into a paste and chill so that the flavors become well intermingled. This is also used to sauce plain spaghetti. Serves lots. Good dish for cocktail parties where a few guests stay on and on and on.

Balkan eggplant casserole

TIME: 1½ HOURS

The people around the Mediterranean who cook eggplant so imaginatively and well think that lamb and eggplant are an inseparable combination. Certainly it seems so in many of the dishes.

Menu: COLD JELLIED CONSOMMÉ
BALKAN EGGPLANT CASSEROLE
HOT GARLIC BREAD
BOWL OF FRESH BLACK BING CHERRIES WITH STEMS LEFT
ON
COFFEE

BALKAN EGGPLANT CASSEROLE:

1 eggplant, peeled and cut crosswise ½-inch-thick slices
1 large onion or 2 medium, cut in ¼-inch-thick slices
3 large or 4 medium tomatoes, sliced
2 green peppers, seeds removed and cut in strips
Salt and pepper
2 cups chopped cooked lamb
¼ cup olive oil
4 eggs, beaten with more salt and pepper

Take a casserole with a tightly fitting cover and butter it well. Put a layer of eggplant, onion, tomatoes, pepper, lamb, salt and pepper and sprinkle generously with olive oil. Repeat the layers until all the ingredients are used. Cover and bake in a medium (350°) oven ¾ to 1 hour. Remove from the oven, uncover, pour the beaten eggs over the eggplant mixture very quickly, cover, and put back in oven 10 or 15 minutes or until the eggs are cooked custard-fashion. Serves 4.

Beaten beans (fasole batuta—Roumanian)

TIME: 12 TO 24 HOURS

These beans, strangely enough, are a rather delicate dish. They are cooked the usual way, and then beaten until light and fluffy.

Menu: DEERFOOT SAUSAGE OR CHORIZO, THE HOT SPANISH SAUSAGE
        FASOLE BATUTA
        SLIM STALKS OF BELGIAN ENDIVE WITH A SMALL BOWL OF
           SALTED AND PEPPERED OLIVE OIL TO DIP IN
        SALTY RYE
        STEWED DRIED APRICOTS SPRINKLED WITH SLIVERED AL-
          MONDS

FASOLE BATUTA:
    1 pound marrow-fat beans, soaked overnight
    Olive oil
    Salt and pepper
    2 medium-sized onions, chopped fine
    More olive oil

Cover the soaked beans with fresh water and simmer until tender or until the skin curls back when a few beans are blown upon. Drain and put through a potato ricer or food mill. Whip and add in a little warm olive oil bit by bit. Pile into a casserole and sprinkle with the chopped onions, sautéed in olive oil until crisp. Put in oven 15 or 20 minutes. Serve hot. Serves 4 generously.

Swiss sauerkraut

TIME: 3 HOURS OR MORE

In Switzerland the sauerkraut is cooked slowly with pork, bacon, wine, and juniper berries. The longer it cooks the more mellow it becomes and the better it is. This bears no relation at all to the sharp, harsh sauerkraut served with hot dogs here. It is served with boiled potatoes on top, along with knackwurst and frankfurters. Each person is served a slice of each kind of pork. This is similar to the Alsatian *choucroute garnie*.

Menu: SWISS SAUERKRAUT
       SOUR RYE BREAD
       APRICOT TART
       COFFEE

SWISS SAUERKRAUT:

> 3 onions, boiled briefly and sliced thin
> 2 tablespoons bacon drippings or other fat
> ½ pound salt pork, in one piece, parboiled 15 minutes
> ¼ pound bacon, in one piece, parboiled 15 minutes
> 2 pounds sauerkraut, fresh if possible
> 1 cup white wine
> Salt
> 7 or 8 peppercorns
> 1 bay leaf
> 1 dozen juniper berries
> Boiled potatoes
> Frankfurters (fat garlic kind, cooked separately)
> Knackwurst, cooked separately

Sauté the onion in the bacon drippings, in the bottom of a deep, heavy pan, such as a Dutch oven. Add the pork and brown it. Then add the boiled bacon and salt pork. Rinse the sauerkraut, if you like it mild, and squeeze out with the fingers, then pull apart so it's not too lumped. Add the sauerkraut to the meat, onions, the wine, salt and peppercorns, bay leaf, juniper berries. Cover and simmer for two or three hours; it can't be overcooked. This tastes even better the next day when reheated. Top with potatoes, the frankfurters, and knackwurst. Serves 6 to 8.

Spaghetti with fresh herbs (Italian)

TIME: 30 MINUTES IF COOKED, 1 HOUR IF CHILLED

In the Genoa region of Italy spaghetti is sauced simply and well with handfuls of fresh basil and parsley simmered in butter into a pale green cream. Some cream the garlic, basil, parsley, chopped fine, and butter ahead of time, instead of cooking it, and chill, giving the herbs time to permeate the butter. This herb butter, called *pesto* (see instructions at end of recipe for minestrone, page 203), is put in lumps on the hot pasta. Both ways are good.

Menu: HOT MUSHROOM BOUILLON
       SPAGHETTI WITH FRESH HERBS
       SLICED TOMATOES
       FRENCH OR ITALIAN BREAD
       CHEESECAKE
       COFFEE

SPAGHETTI WITH FRESH HERBS:
1 medium onion, minced
4 cloves garlic, minced
1 stick (¼ pound) sweet butter
¼ cup olive oil
4 tablespoons chopped fresh basil or 2 dried
¼ cup finely chopped parsley
¼ cup more butter
Grated Parmesan cheese
1 pound pasta of any shape (the shell is pretty), cooked
*   in salted boiling water until tender but not mushy*

Sauté the onion and garlic in the butter, add the olive oil, basil, and parsley. Simmer for about 5 minutes. Add 1 cup water and simmer for 20 minutes more. Just before serving add the rest of the butter. Serve the grated Parmesan at the table in its own bowl, to be sprinkled on the top. Serves 4 generously.

Soup with tiny meat balls (polpette—Italian)

TIME: 50 MINUTES

The *polpette* are the very tiny and simplified meat balls that float in many Italian soups. About 4 or 5 should be in each bowl.

Menu: SOUP WITH TINY MEAT BALLS
> COOKED GREEN BEANS, MARINATED IN FRENCH DRESSING (2 PARTS OLIVE OIL, 1 PART GARLIC VINEGAR, SALT AND PEPPER), DRAIN AND SPRINKLE WITH CHOPPED BLACK WALNUTS
>
> FRENCH OR ITALIAN BREAD
>
> SOUR CHERRY PIE
>
> COFFEE

SOUP WITH TINY MEAT BALLS:
Soup:
> 2 cups beef broth
> 1 carrot, scraped and chopped fine
> 3 potatoes, peeled and chopped
> 3 stalks celery, tops and bottoms chopped
> Orégano
> Salt and pepper
> ½ cup fine soup pasta
> 4 tablespoons canned tomatoes
> Grated Parmesan cheese

Polpette:
> 1 pound lean beef, ground
> 1 whole egg
> 1 clove garlic, minced
> 2 slices bread, soaked in water, and then squeezed out
> Salt and pepper
> 2 tablespoons butter

For the broth simmer beef broth, carrot, potatoes and celery, orégano, salt and pepper together for 20 to 30 minutes. For the polpette mix the beef, egg, garlic, bread, salt and pepper and make into tiny meat balls about the size of a red button radish. Sauté in butter. Drop the polpette and any fine soup pasta into the soup. Cook about 2 minutes more and serve in bowls with the grated Parmesan to sprinkle on top. Serves 4.

Lamb with tomatoes (kouzou kzartma—Armenian)

TIME: 1 HOUR, 40 MINUTES

This is one of the many, and good, ways the people around the Mediterranean cook lamb, yet it is fairly simple to prepare.

Menu: KOUZOU KZARTMA
PRESSED CUCUMBERS (see menu, page 168)
CORN BREAD
SPONGECAKE SPREAD THICKLY WITH WHIPPED CREAM AND
SPRINKLED WITH CRUSHED PEANUT BRITTLE
COFFEE

KOUZOU KZARTMA:
6 lamb shoulder chops
1 small can tomatoes
Salt and paprika
10 tiny new potatoes, boiled separately and peeled

Rinse the meat (this is the Armenian way), put in a shallow casserole with the tomatoes, 1 cup water, salt and paprika. Bake in a 350° oven, 1½ hours. Fifteen minutes before serving add the boiled and peeled potatoes. Serves 4 to 6.

Rognons flambé (French)

TIME: 15 MINUTES

Anywhere but here kidneys are loved, esteemed, and cooked imaginatively as in this dish.

Menu: COLD TOMATO AND POTATO SOUP (FOR A SIMPLIFIED VERSION BLEND ONION RINGS SAUTÉED UNTIL ALMOST CARAMELIZED, TOMATO SOUP, VICHYSSOISE, CHILLED AND SPRINKLED WITH CHOPPED FRESH CHERVIL)
ROGNONS FLAMBÉ
RISI PISI (RICE COOKED IN CHICKEN BROTH WITH A CUP OF COOKED FRESH PEAS AND A GENEROUS AMOUNT OF BUTTER)
TOAST CIRCLES (USE A COOKY CUTTER OR GLASS)
HONEYDEW MELON (HALVES OR BALLS), LIME ICE, AND FRESH RASPBERRIES

ROGNONS FLAMBÉ:
2 veal kidneys
2 tablespoons sweet butter
1 jigger brandy
Salt and pepper
1 teaspoon dry English mustard or 1 tablespoon Dijon or other prepared mustard
1 tablespoon heavy cream
1 tablespoon more sweet butter
1 tablespoon lemon juice

Cut the kidneys in pieces at the sections and cut off the white membrane or fat and discard. Sauté the kidneys briefly in butter until brown on all sides, about 3 or 4 minutes. Add the brandy and light with a match. When the flames die down, add the salt and pepper, mustard, heavy cream, and the rest of the sweet butter. Simmer for about 5 minutes. Add the lemon juice very slowly to prevent curdling. Serve immediately on circles of toast. Serves 4.

Ham and noodles (schinkenfleckerl—Czechoslovakian)

TIME: 50 MINUTES

The Czechoslovakians, like the Germans, are fond of such robust and filling food as noodles and put almost any meat with it. However, the meat is most apt to be ham or pork.

Menu: SCHINKENFLECKERL
SALAD: GREENS, TOMATOES, CHOPPED GREEN ONIONS, AND SLICED RADISHES, SLICED CUCUMBERS WITH FRENCH DRESSING (2 PARTS OLIVE OIL, 1 PART GARLIC VINEGAR, SALT AND PEPPER)
HOT SALT STICKS, BROWN-AND-SERVE KIND
BROWN BETTY
COFFEE

SCHINKENFLECKERL:
½ pound noodles, cooked in boiling salted water until tender but not mushy
1 pound diced cooked ham, or chopped cooked beef
1 cup evaporated milk (heavy cream may be used, but Mrs. Li, who grew up in Czechoslovakia, likes the texture that evaporated milk gives the dish)
Salt and pepper
3 tablespoons grated cheese, preferably Parmesan or Romano

Mix the cooked, drained noodles with the chopped ham or beef and milk, salt and pepper. Turn into a buttered, shallow casserole and sprinkle the grated cheese on top. Bake in a 350° oven until the crust is light brown. Serves 4.

Boulgour with leban or sour cream (Mediterranean)

TIME: 45 MINUTES

Cracked wheat, which may be bought ground fine, medium, or coarse, is a flavorful and nutty food used often, as rice is in many of the Mediterranean or Asia Minor countries. It is available in many groceries catering to a foreign population and, somewhat depressingly, health-food stores.

Menu: BROILED CHICKEN BASTED WITH BUTTER AND TARRAGON
BOULGOUR WITH LEBAN OR SOUR CREAM
CUCUMBER AND ONION ASPIC
HOT DROP BISCUITS
COLD FRESH PLUMS
COFFEE

BOULGOUR WITH LEBAN OR SOUR CREAM:
 ¼ cup olive oil
 1 cup boulgour, medium-ground
 2 cups boiling salted water
 1 cup leban (the name for yoghurt in the Near East), or
  1 cup sour cream

Heat the olive oil in a large, heavy skillet, add the boulgour, and stir over a low flame. Watch carefully, stirring constantly until all is a golden brown. Transfer the boulgour to the boiling water, cover, and cook until the water is absorbed but the boulgour is not soggy. Heat again in the oiled skillet just to make sure. Serve with yoghurt or sour cream. Serves 4.

Pizza layered with Swiss chard (Italian)

TIME: 1½ HOURS

Just as no two literate Italians I have known, and there have been many, spell any word alike, no two Italians I know cook anything exactly alike. While this resembles a pizza, and is called so, it isn't just the same, with its two layers and its green filling.

Menu: PIZZA LAYERED WITH SWISS CHARD
BELGIAN TOMATO SALAD (see page 98)
LEMON SHERBET SPRINKLED WITH CHOCOLATE CHIPS
COFFEE

PIZZA LAYERED WITH SWISS CHARD:
2 thin layers of pizza dough (see page 94) or use a hot-roll mix
1½ cups chopped, cooked Swiss chard
1 fat clove garlic, or 2 thin ones, minced
3 tablespoons olive oil
Salt and pepper
4 or 5 anchovies, cut into 2 or 3 pieces

Spread one circle or square, whichever you wish, of the dough with the Swiss chard mixed with the garlic sautéed in the olive oil. Dot the pieces of anchovies around and add the top layer. Bake in an oven at 450° to 500° or top heat for 15 minutes until brown. Serve hot or cold. Serves 4.

For the girls
From Fort Mill

INDEX

216

217

219

DATE DUE

MAY 2 8 '69			
AUG 1 '69			
MAY 2 8 '71			
NOV 11 '75			
APR. 25.1985			
SEP 3 1990			
OCT 1 1990			
GAYLORD			PRINTED IN U.S.A.